DATE DUE

#47-0108 Peel Off Pressure Sensitive

Moths in the Memory

Moths
in the
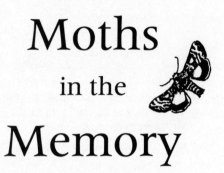
Memory
a postwar spring

JAMES

BIRDSALL

PAVILION

First published in Great Britain in 1990 by
PAVILION BOOKS LIMITED
196 Shaftesbury Avenue, London WC2H 8JL

Text and illustrations copyright © 1990 James Birdsall

Designed by Peter Guy

A CIP catalogue record for this book is
available from the British Library

ISBN 1 85145 451 9

10 9 8 7 6 5 4 3 2 1

Typeset by Wyvern Typesetting, Bristol
Printed and bound in Great Britain by
Billings and Son Limited

Contents

Preface, 7

Acknowledgements

The author would like to thank Mrs Jocelyn Starling for her kind permission to reproduce one of the late Timothy Birdsall's drawings. His thanks go also to Bernard Levin and to *The Times* for their kind permission to quote separate passages in this book, and to Jocelyn and to BBC Television for permission to revive a sample of Tim's text as broadcast on the BBC Television series, *That Was the Week That Was* in 1963.

Death's Head Hawk moth

Preface

Old Jim was scathing.

'Tha can't call it "Moths in 'Mem'ry"!'

'"Moths in *the* Memory." Why not?'

'Sounds like tha mem'ry's full of girt 'oles!'

'Ah! Well, that's the clever bit. A sort of *double entendre*.'

'Hey up! Doobalong what?'

'Tendre. French remark.'

'Nay! What d'you want laikin' about wi' French remarks? Is there owt about Yorkshire in it?'

'Yes. Much more about Yorkshire.'

''Appen that'll help. Bit o' good Yorkshire'll settle ony amount o' doobalongs.'

'Laiking', for the enlightenment of those unfamiliar with the local patois, is directly synonymous with 'playing', as in 'laikin' dominoes', or simply 'laikin' about'. It is also the opposite of 'working'. Its etymology is obscure (to me at ony road), lost in the ancient mists of the Dales when the Phantom Hound roamed Troller's Ghyll and Boggarts lurked nastily in every pot-hole. 'Outdated superstition,' we scoff patronizingly from the comfort of the bar parlour, or feet stretched out to the blaze of the realistic gas glow from our pseudo, hygienic log fire – but up there alone as the mizzle sets in and the forlorn curlews complain and the visible horizon shrinks to the accumulating droplets on the wild thyme and marjoram at our feet, we wish uneasily, like frightened children at bedtime, that nobody had ever told us the story.

The Yorkshire dialect, which is not the same thing as the accent, is a composite language of its own (even the 'thees' and 'thous', if you listen, are used grammatically). When I was a boy, the old-timers were unwittingly bi-lingual, and would adapt their language to suit the listener. There are few of them left today and only the occasional word or phrase crops up in conversation. My present critic added to the confusion of a carload of disoriented tourists who had come through the village vainly seeking a peaceful short cut from the busy main road below. It was the August bank holiday and they were looking for the Lake District, some forty miles north. 'Tha's coom to the reight place!' crowed my friend reassuringly. 'They're all ruddy laikin' round here!'

My story is not confined to Yorkshire, that rugged, insular province which, though the biggest of the English counties, is also arguably the smallest parish. The habitats of my brothers and myself, and the moths we pursued and cherished, ranged from the northerly Dales through Hertfordshire south to Sussex, two other counties which we roamed and loved. We knew a London in our day which has changed immeasurably, where boys and girls were safe to explore unmolested, policemen stood by most of the traffic lights ready with directions or the time of day, and bus tickets in a range of pretty colours were dispensed by the conductor, with a musical ring, off a board, to which they were secured by mousetrap clips.

Our schooldays were spent in Yorkshire, close to roots which have reclaimed me for the past thirty years, but home and the holidays were in the south. With a foot planted firmly in each camp, we felt that we could speak for either with a personal authority. When in the north we used to defend the reputed indolence of the southerner and his unsportsmanlike habit of co-opting alien hirelings to represent his county at cricket; when at home, we would champion the northerner's bluntness and refusal to acknowledge the validity of any culture but his own. Yorkshiremen on holiday thoroughly enjoy a continuous grumble and can't wait to get back home. Eastbourne was always full of them, and we would eavesdrop nostalgically from behind as they walked the promenade. 'Call that a kipper they gave us this morning? I could have soled my boots with it, they're getting a bit thin – and that's another thing . . .'

My spectacles – I didn't need them in those days – are just possibly rose-tinted, but not distorting. As more villages become incidental points en route to bypass or motorway, as their pubs adapt to cater for the passing trade, as I see our England evolving into a land not so much of beauty as of beauty-spots, and the scant remaining stone barns waiting around, like the heathen of old, to be 'converted', I have an urge to get down some picture of what it used to be like. Not out of despair or nostalgia or resentment, but simply before I forget. Time passes so quickly, and indeed accelerates. As old Jim says at the domino table, as he shuffles the bones with a rattle, 'Enough chat! Coom on, get laikin'!'

JAS BIRDSALL
Yorkshire 1989

1

Metropolis
and Market Town

Eyed Hawk moth

I MUST HAVE BEEN RISING FOUR YEARS OLD WHEN TIM AND I, TO our embarrassed shame in later years, were once frightened by a large moth. I have since learned to temper lay estimates of the size of moths. An excited, often hysterical, cry of 'There's a *huge* moth in the loo!' – or the hall or the kitchen – would in my salad days have fetched me at the double, with visions of a fine Hawk moth or at the least a well proportioned, gaudy Tiger. Usually it would turn out to be a Magpie moth or a Silver 'Y', about two inches in wingspan at most, who had ventured in because of the light and was just as anxious to escape as was the alarmist. It's rather like fishermen's gauges of weight and length. Divide by four and you're likely to be about right.

This, however, was a categorically large moth. We were breaking the journey from London to Yorkshire, and my brother and I (Patrick was not yet born) were sharing a bed in the 'Ram Jam Inn' which stood about half-way. The moth had come in through the open window, attracted by the lamp, and flew in wide, swift circles around the room. As there was no question of turning the light out with such a disturbing bedfellow, Dad went into action, eventually succeeded in catching it in a tumbler and, to allay our fears, showed it to us. I recall gaudily painted 'eyes'. Later, when we knew more about such things, we calculated that it must have been either an Eyed Hawk, which has two on the hindwings, or an Empress, which has four beautiful eyes, one on each wing. Both span a good three inches and have thick, furry bodies. The moth was duly released through the window and we settled down, but the image remains vividly with me to this day.

I am not one to scoff at those who are scared of moths, beyond pointing out that they are essentially gentle creatures and entirely harmless. Fear of spiders I can readily understand, though I rather like them. Daddy-long-legs, the Crane flies, known almost onomatopoeically in Yorkshire as 'Jinnie-spinners', have a similarly malevolent legginess. The Rev. M. R. James, ghost story writer supreme, wrote his most spine-chilling story about Daddy-long-legs. Even the fear of bats has a certain wild logic, though the origin of the time-honoured myth that they delight in getting tangled up in your hair long defeated my imagination. I now suspect that in the days of Hardy's Tess, wild tressed milkmaids coming home over the fields at dusk, each with her attendant little cloud of gnats and midges dancing above her head, may have attracted the feeding bats which would occasionally swoop too close for comfort. I am often 'dive-bombed' by swallows on an evening's fishing, but it's not me they're after.

All things that creep or crawl or buzz about present a possible menace, with however little foundation. But I have a totally irrational fear of toy balloons, which is why I am so blandly tolerant of others' more explicable phobias. A calm man am I, stolid, pipe puffing, insensitive alike to irritant and atmosphere, but a balloon provokes in me the reaction which traditionally a mouse arouses in the elephant. Limp and inert, balloons offer no threat. I can stare boldly at them for hours. Even fully expanded they can be faced with equanimity, except when people produce that alarming rasping sound by kneading them with the thumbs. It is the sight of a balloon being blown up that engenders my real terror. This was a considerable embarrassment when the children were young and I would have to leave a party, sweating, and be quietly sick in the garden. Children, other people's, are allowed to be sick at parties – it's a backhanded compliment to the irresistible fare provided, like belching at a Middle-Eastern feast – but not adults. I was taken as a child to Bertram Mills' Circus. It must have been early in the war, as we were wearing what Mr Churchill had christened 'siren suits'. To my agony one grotesque clown sat on the floor blowing up huge balloons until they burst. That I managed to sit out the show was a triumph of self-discipline.

Moths, then, no longer worried me from that day on. They have occupied much of my time and thoughts throughout my life, often when both should have been devoted to graver and more weighty matters, as when trying to concentrate on mathematical concepts or patrolling the outfield at cricket. Those who have read my earlier book will remember how my brothers, Tim and Patrick, and I were preoccupied with the butterflies. Alongside them flew the moths. There just wasn't room for them in the first volume. Here is still a world of fascination; of intricate aerodynamic structure that engineering skill has yet to emulate; of wondrous, seemingly abstract design that Art can but clumsily attempt to follow; of behavioural patterns and genetic complexity that will intrigue the biologists for centuries to come, and, above all, for boys with more energies than responsibilities, of absorbing application, sound exercise and very good fun.

As the 1930s moved to their end and my conscious memories were starting to accumulate – though I was blissfully unconscious of the uneasy rumblings at home and in Europe – we were living in

Kensington. The rural aspect of life then was supplied largely by regular visits to my grandparents in Yorkshire. True, we spent part of most fine afternoons in Kensington Gardens, hardly bucolic but the next best thing, in a world that has vanished even more surely than the dog-and-stick farmland into which we were to become so integrated. It is the fashion and the social structure of the time that have become extinct. Nature has a way of waiting quietly with an awesome patience to move back and claim its own.

The pictures I retain now seem curiously like a euphoric evocation of the Edwardian era, peopled by prams and still uniformed nannies, punctuated by visits to the Peter Pan statue and the Elfin Oak and feeding the ducks on the Round Pond. There was the melancholy keeper, also in uniform, who wandered about with a pointed stick, rather spiritlessly spiking up discarded paper bags and orange peel. When the stick was clogged with litter right to the top, a long, unappetizing kebab, he would scrape it off on the edge of a convenient bin like a desultory swordsman and amble off in another direction. We wore leggings, like Christopher Robin, and those dreadful sun-hats and there were hoops and toy boats and whip-and-top. From itinerant pedlars you could buy colourful little windmills on sticks which whizzed round gaily as you ran, and strange fluttering pink and yellow birds on a string which flapped and churred noisily in the breeze.

There were squirrels in the park, usually spreadeagled on a tree trunk, deftly scuttling out of sight to the other side, and then back again when you tiptoed round to look. Most of the garden birds were there. Of course one should say 'woodland' birds, for that is what they really are, though happily they have colonized our gardens as an acceptable substitute. Woodpigeons kept to the trees in the main, though an occasional one would come for crumbs, his white-ringed neck conspicuous among the duller plumage of the crowds of London pigeons scuttling busily at one's feet for bread and split peas. At picnics I would always make off with the small cruet, chasing the elusive birds. Something magical would happen if you managed to put salt and pepper on a pigeon's tail. As I never achieved this feat, the aim still remains a mystery.

The sleepily insistent five-note call of the brooding woodpigeons ('take *two* sticks, Taffy!') always recalls days in the park, even though I hear it now in a more natural environment. I am regularly niggled when watching an otherwise scrupulously researched period play on the television (the skill with which they do these things often distracts me from the drama). The scene, say, a carriage sweep; peacocks on the lawn; ladies shawled and parasolled, maybe a game of croquet and earnest young men in boaters and flannels. Never a drone of a passing Pan-Am jet nor strident siren of distant police car jars one back into our noisy present. And then, among the idyllic background of birdsong and the clack of mallets, comes the (three-note) cooing of the collared dove. Oh, calamity! as Robertson Hare used to exclaim emotionally. The Eastern immigrant didn't get here till about twenty years ago! Such anachronism jolts me with all the force of a zip fastener on a mediaeval doublet.

Many treats are marred for me by my pernickety mind. Suspension of disbelief should be a willing compact, not a discipline, but sometimes it requires an effort. Oscar Wilde's fairy stories are a joy to me. I weep for the swallow and the Happy Prince. I boil with indignation at the selfishness of Big Hugh the Miller. Loveliest of all, in imagery and lush description, is the tale of the Nightingale and the Rose. All night long, with her breast against a thorn, the nightingale pours out her song that a white rose may become stained red with her heart's blood to comply with the whim of a love-sick student. *Her* song? Sadly, Mr Wilde, it is only the male nightingale who sings. His lady is no songstress and the story is as spurious as your green carnation.

Kensington Gardens would probably have provided a good hunting ground for caterpillars and moths, but the craze hadn't gripped me in those days and I gave them only passing notice. I remember following a caterpillar round the flagged edge of the Round Pond. It was in a hurry, with that wave-like humping movement many hairy caterpillars develop when they are urgently seeking somewhere to spin a cocoon. It was black, with a gold stripe down the length of the back, which identifies it, even at this distance, as a White Ermine moth, common enough but handsome all the same. I didn't take it home but, after heading it away from the water, I left it to its search.

The park gave me my earliest impressions of the changing seasons. Autumn brought the musty smells of fallen leaves, the keeper's acrid little bonfires and the noisy trudging of wellington boots through the debris to knock out the conkers. Or more rarely the urchinesque seed balls of the plane trees which I greatly coveted. They seemed to hang on to their parents with limpet tenacity and were invariably out of reach above. Winter was desolate, a time of constant chiding for lost gloves and sitting on deserted swings or those cumbersome cast iron horses – three or four seaters – which rocked heavily fore and aft when shoved by an adult from behind, but stubbornly refused to budge for the three of us unaided. They had sullen, moulded iron faces which reflected their souls.

Summer was busy with life and the bands played and the bustle was infectious. There were metal drinking cups chained to the ornamental Victorian fountains, but we were forbidden ever to use them on grounds of hygiene. Earlier the spring had brought the changes and promise which stir me still today, but then bordered on the magical. Perversely it is not the natural world of 'Spring in the Park' that prods my memory the most, but a brilliant fantasy of the *Punch* artist and editor, Fougasse. He pictured the park chairs – those archetypal chairs of folding iron rods and wooden slats – in the rutting season. The chairs prance and pose and eventually do battle, head-rests locked like antlers, until the defeated one limps away and the victor strikes a magnificent attitude on a mound, as though posing for Landseer.

'The Monarch of the Glen' brings me back to Yorkshire, for a darkly framed print of this beast, with his human eyes, hung in my little white room in Raikes Lea, the Skipton home of my grand-parents. The house was in a cul-de-sac up the 'Raikes', epitome of Yorkshire Dales place-names. Landseer's stag contrasted, rather oddly I suppose, with a nursery frieze of Disney's Three Little Pigs prancing above the picture rail. Not that it bothered me. It bothered Tim, however, who often shared the bed with me under its patch-work quilt. Not the aesthetics of the thing, but the grim and repetitive Big Bad Wolf, who figured about five times below the coving. Sticking single prints of Mickey Mouse and Donald Duck over the lupine ogre diminished Tim's nightmares to some extent, but the horror that you can't see is often more frightening than the one you can. Indeed I knew something which nobody else had spotted: that in the shadows above a mahogany wardrobe he could still be seen. They had missed that one. I didn't tell Tim for years.

Other Victorian pot-boilers hung on the walls. There was a wistful little girl in a pinny gazing at a robin, and another depicting a small boy in a crumpled sailor suit, surrounded by malevolent-looking barnyard fowls and labelled 'No Safety Anywhere!' The window overlooked a lovely garden and an immaculate lawn, as smooth as baize and jealously protected. Beyond the garden wall were the vegetable plots of the Union Workhouse, soon to evolve into a hospital, after which the ground would be raked and hoed by soldiers in bright blue uniforms, casualties of the war. More distantly lay the Aire Valley and the London, Midland and Scottish Railway, source of cheerful shunting noises, hoots and whistles which competed with the dawn chorus of birdsong when I lay awake, waiting for the house to start stirring and the day to begin. A rise above the town, where a recreation ground footed the sprawling slopes of Rombalds Moor, was crested by a clump of trees forming the unmistakable silhouette of a goat. The first ritual on arrival for a visit was to rush upstairs to look at the Goat.

The day began – long days they are when you are five and into everything – when I heard Gramp beginning to move about. Throughout his long life he would rise well before six to light the kitchen fire and provide tea at seven for everyone who happened to be staying – the only domestic chores he performed. Subsequent cooking, cleaning and washing-up were women's work, and demarcation lines were rigid. On reflection there could have been an element of mischief in the seven-o'clock tea delivery, for he nursed lofty scorn for those who couldn't get up in the morning. I, on the other hand, am far more indulgent. A reluctant morning riser since childhood, I have no objection to other people getting up as early as they like. I only demur when they make a sham virtue out of necessity and take up a holier-than-me attitude about it.

Gramp would be half dressed, with a pair of Turkish slippers and a black velvet smoking jacket, going rather green in its advanced years. I would perch comfortably on his knee in front of the fire and we would solve a daily mathematical puzzle posed by (yesterday's) *Yorkshire Post*, dealing with trains going at different speeds or bluebottles crossing diagonally inside a box. He must have applied the Socratic theory that if you ask the right questions you can extract the right answer from any student, for I understood them then as surely as I have forgotten them now. The next ritual was watching him shave, walking about with a mug of boiling water, steaming cloths, much lather and twists of tissue paper and a set of cut-throat razors which were sharpened rhythmically on a leather strop. I would follow every movement apprehensively as his face emerged from the soap, a little more at every rectangular scrape, until the last snowy wisps disappeared into a towel. The skill involved in coming unscathed through the ordeal impressed me anew every morning.

The kitchen was not to be confused with the adjacent scullery, where the cooking and washing-up took place. A large white-scrubbed wooden table dominated the room, perpetually covered with an autumnally toned plush cloth, soft but stubbly under your fingers, except on baking or ironing days. No flimsy, collapsible ironing board this, but a sturdy slab which would take half a double sheet at a time. The job was done with an electric iron, but two flat irons still sat solidly in the hearth as though their day might yet come round again.

In our kitchen today, scarcely a quarter of the size, many of the items, functional then, are hung up like bruised arms, for ornaments if not for monuments. Cane carpet beater and stone hot water bottle; brass jam pans, a copper colander and old shuttles festoon the walls and beams. Copper measuring jugs hang above us on long handles. Stone flour jars, cooking pots and brass weighing scales top the cupboards and, elsewhere in the house, an inherited selection of decorated ewers and basins are filled with pot-pourri and stand at tilted angles.

There are no more lumber rooms today where yesterday's ephemera can be stored until fashion once more welcomes them a generation or two hence. But hang on to your copper ballcocks, deposed coffee percolators, ashtrays and cigarette lighters and crown cork bottle openers and hoard anything plastic from dolls to dustbin liners, for one day the oil will run out from the Virgins' lamps and the Sheikhs' great fields and these items will be hung in your great grandchildren's kitchens – or dining-microwave-dens, for cooking as such will be a nostalgic indulgence, much as peeling potatoes is now.

Just one century ago, in 1889, Jerome K. Jerome published his *Three Men in a Boat* and sang the same prophetic song:

> Will it be the same in the future? Will the prized treasures of today always be the cheap trifles of the day before? Will rows of our Willow-pattern dinner-plates be ranged above the chimney pieces of the great in the years 2000 and odd? Will the white cups with the gold rim and the beautiful gold flowers inside (species unknown), that our Sarah-Janes now break in sheer light-heartedness of spirit, be carefully mended, and stood upon a bracket, and dusted only by the lady of the house?

The answer needs no elaboration.

The kitchen table provided a playground and work surface of infinite versatility once breakfast was cleared away. The meal would start solemnly enough with the eight-o'clock news, when none dared speak, for the anticipatory fuse which had spluttered in the background of our earliest years had exploded into the dreadful reality of a world war. The post, laid out in front of Gramp's comfortable Windsor chair (we had stools, known in Yorkshire as buffets), was opened in silence. Letters were slit with a smooth ivory knife. Parcels had every knot carefully undone and the string meticulously looped and stored in the string drawer in the solid pine dresser. Eventually the head of the table retired behind the *Yorkshire Post*, a signal that the meeting was declared informal, and long-pent tongues were loosed.

Later the table would be covered in paintboxes, jigsaws or plasticine, caterpillar jars for cleaning and feeding, or small mayflies on moss in a jam-jar; for the mayfly, unlike butterflies and moths, has a further moult in the winged stage and changes from a 'dun' to a handsome 'spinner', and we thrilled to watch. There were lead soldiers (mostly from previous wars), battleships, zoo animals (my favourites) or games of draughts or halma and a beautiful circular solitaire board with exquisite marbles incredibly full of coloured filigree and delicate spirals of lace. Other treasures included a kaleidoscope and a gyroscope, wound with a string, which perched swaying on a knife edge and never fell off. Supervised at weekends, we would peer down the microscope at protozoa from the bird-bath or cheese mites, big as hogs, clambering in the dust from the rind of the Stilton in the pantry. Often the table would be completely covered in feathers and silks while Gramp spent an hour or two replenishing his stock of trout flies, a craft into which I was initiated at an early age.

High on the wall above the table in a glazed box was one of those fascinating indicator panels with rows of brass stars which wobbled whenever a bell was pressed in the house, and were labelled 'Front Door' and 'Housekeeper' (there wasn't one) and 'Dining Room' and such. There was even a bell push above the bath – disconnected when we were staying as we couldn't keep our fingers off it. I asked Dad why there should be a bell in the bathroom, and he told me it was for Morsing instructions about breakfast to the cook. Everywhere were mundane objects of unusual interest. A tab rug, of muted black and dull beige, lay in front of the hearth, made, I was told, of old stockings. I avoided treading on it in bare feet as it made me think uneasily of old legs. High on the ceiling, attached to a cleat by a rope and pulley, swung a rack for clothes drying, known as a 'Tidy Betty'. This nickname was also a pet name for the dunnock, the little hedge sparrow who never grabbed any of the crumbs from the bird table, but searched about underneath on the flagstones, delicately picking at minute specks which hardly seemed to provide an adequate meal.

One could tell what day it was by the smells. Monday was washing day and smelt of bleach and soda, the stinging smell of ammonia and the sweet smell of ironed linen. The yeasty flavour of the brewery proclaimed it Tuesday or Friday, for bread was baked twice a week and the work started early. It is a curious fact that, although among our atrophied human senses the disused sense of smell has probably suffered the greatest eclipse since we evolved more sophisticated and less natural means of communication, yet scents and smells remain the most vivid involuntary goads to the memory. A remembered tune, a particular phrase, a forgotten landmark can recall the past, but a smell can shock us into an unbidden memory with abrupt, unexpected clarity.

My grandparents' home had a scent compounded of lavender, wood smoke, rare roast beef and grilled trout. The components varied in ascendancy as you moved about the house, and other, minor themes became apparent in specific places. The smell of transparent Pears soap pervaded the bathroom; a strangely male smell when you consider the advertising copy since Millais and 'Bubbles'. In the pantry in the cellar below the stairs it was ham which predominated. Hams hanging up as solid as wood. Snipe, wild duck, grouse, blackcock, partridge and pheasant hung there in their season, feathered and gamily redolent. Ripe and mellow cheeses added to the atmosphere on a huge subterranean stone slab where we half expected to see stalactites. As children we were intrigued how some smells were pleasant, even exciting, without being flavours we had any wish to taste. Among these we listed the smells of tar and of rubber, the clean smells of petrol and of ether and the musty smell of old books. A good cigar smells better than it tastes, and good coffee infinitely more so.

The rest of the house was spacious but not really our domain. Doors were solid and mysterious, covered as they were with heavy plush curtains hung from ingenious Victorian rails which rose up as the door opened, lifting the curtain clear of the floor. This revealed a sectioned roller at the base. Central heating was unknown, and draught prevention in the chilly North called out all man's invention. A warm bedroom was considered 'a bit soft'. Really cold weather was marked by the startling announcement, 'I think we'll light the fire in the Breakfast Room'. This beautiful room was never used for breakfast, in fact rarely used at all. However, it was scrupulously cleaned every day and 'bottomed' once a week, which involved getting out every mote of dust from under the heavier pieces of furniture such as the piano.

Piano practice involved the removal of shoes, as we couldn't reach the pedals, and toes would kick involuntarily against polished rosewood. Dominating the room, under a ceiling delicately painted to represent sky and clouds, hung a huge Joseph Farquharson painting of sheep in the snow with a luminous evening sun filtering amber lights and blue shadows through bare winter trees. I have known the painting all my life, but it is only in recent years that I have seen similar work by the same artist. Displays of Christmas cards and art shop prints are now fully sprinkled with Farquharsons, all of sheep in snow.

Paintings and prints hung all over the house, mostly landscapes spanning Yorkshire from the crag at Kilnsey to the coast at Whitby. Some in the sitting-room which always took my eye were by the late A.R. Smith, a local friend and an inspired artist. In recent years water-colour painting has become something of a cottage industry in the Dales, some of it good and much perfunctory, but no artist I have ever known has been able to capture the pale ochreous-hazel tones of Wharfedale in late winter as did Reginald Smith.

A perfect cornucopia of pictures was provided by the contents of the massive bookcase; Thorburn's birds, copiously illustrated Hans Andersen and Grimm, lovingly compiled Victorian scrap-books and bound copies of children's magazines of a similar vintage with strictly moral serial stories such as 'The Boy Among the Birds' (a sick child who was somehow transformed into a cock-robin), 'Beyond the Blue Mountains' (a sort of children's *Pilgrim's Progress*) and a surrealist tale entitled 'The Grawlies'. Over the fireplace, keeping stern eyes on decorum, hung a pipe rack with a carved row of cowled monks' heads illustrating the seven deadly sins with sinister accuracy of expression.

These leering guardians would peer at me and past me into the dark hallway, where light percolated above the front door through coloured leaded lights, fashionable in many of the houses in Skipton; strange pendant ovals and fruits in reds and blues, mauves and greens which seemed to me somehow connected with the decorative flasks and bowls then to be seen high in the windows of chemists' shops. A tall pot umbrella stand in the hall was filled with a fascinating range of gamps and home-made walking sticks, and next to it was the dark hall-stand, hung with basket creels and canvas waders, where ritual adjustments of Granny's hats in the mirror were the regular preliminary of a walk into town. I could only consult the mirror by jumping and could never see the spot on the stairs behind my head as it always jumped with me. Upstairs was dark, and haunted – or so we thought – but the banisters were great for sliding down. I hated going upstairs by myself.

Getting out at the front door was problematical as the big stone steps were all too often jealously guarded by Mrs Nutter, scrubbing brush at the ready and a stone for whitening the step edges. 'Tha'll 'ave to coom out t'other way!' Shrugging helplessly we'd trail round to the back door out of the scullery. When not on her knees at the steps, Mrs Nutter was either combing the house for dust with the vacuum cleaner or washing the upstairs windows from ground level with an enormously long-handled brush like the traditional pole of the knocker-up. The steps were rigorously scrubbed every day and were either in the process of being scrubbed or had been lately scrubbed and were still wet. Either way they were inaccessible. If we were lucky and early and Mrs Nutter was in friendly mood, it was 'Coom on then, I've nobbut just started!' and we would scamper thankfully down, though her tone of voice left no doubt as to what a favour was being granted and not to bank on it.

Mrs Nutter was dressed immutably in black, with maybe a touch of dark purple on frivolous days, and with her thick fawn stockings could, like a pheasant on bracken, have lain perfectly camouflaged on the old tab rug. Her invariable greeting in poor weather was 'Morning! Wettintit!' Further conversation consisted of 'Eee!' and 'Nay!' – a range of vocabulary which in Yorkshire can, with care, suffice a person all day and well into the night. I taught my daughter, Deirdre, these invaluable words as the first essentials when she was a mite, and the results were hilarious. In practice, with suitable inflexions, 'Nay!' (or 'Nay?') is a suitable rejoinder to any comment and the 'Eee!' is dispensible.

Once safely out of doors we were free to do as we liked, with certain restrictions. The lawn, when wet, was more strictly out of bounds than the doorstep, but there was a jungle of shrubbery and extensive rockeries where we could burrow and hide all day. Small, furry caterpillars abounded in the ground cover under the bushes; they mostly turned out to be the Knot Grass moth, feeding on the dock and plantains where my grandmother's rapacious weeding had failed to penetrate. When disturbed they would curl up tight and fall in among the roots. By the outside privy grew, doubtless with nice calculation, rows of sweet peas on a trellis. A tiny insect would rise off the plants which we were sure was the Least Pigmy moth, the smallest moth in the British Isles and quite impossible to 'set' for our collection. The loo itself was surrounded by painted matchboard and on each board Gramp had fixed a transfer of the Birds of Britain from a series of Players cigarette cards. They were of a high quality, and to spend half an hour in there was an education in itself.

At some stage in the early 1940s we were introduced to the Yorkshire tradition (well, I've met it nowhere else) of egg rolling at Easter. With friends we would spend hours absorbed in decorating eggs, as intricately if not as expensively as the great Fabergé who did the same job for the Tsars. Did you want overall colour? Hard-boiling with onion skins, blue-bag, beetroot or spinach would stain an egg yellow, blue, red or green respectively, and rhubarb gave a delicate shade of pink. Was it an animal or bird you wished to represent? Pussy willow catkins were glued on for feet or ears, sheep's wool for tails, sycamore seeds for beaks or wings. The results were taken round from house to house for all to see and admire. Then on Easter Sunday we would all climb a hill and roll our eggs down, jumping over root and rock, until at the bottom, the shells suitably shattered, they would be peeled and eaten. They tasted a bit too bland and I would have preferred to keep my squirrel or penguin intact, but I was, after all, in Rome.

The hills were a conspicuous part of the landscape, lacking in our native Hertfordshire, which was fairly flat. (We had by now moved away from London for safety.) Crookrise, romantic name, was the dominant hill. In those days it was forested with broad-leaved woodland of considerable age. Crookrise had its own tribe of rabbits; black ones, white ones and some piebald. A haven for nuthatches, green and spotted woodpeckers and the occasionally glimpsed woodcock and nightjar, the woods gave way to a craggy summit where there was one split in the rock. When found, this gave access to the top and you clambered out to the tewits, redshank and curlews. On the moortop ran a ghyll where a waterfall concealed a cave into which you could climb to eat your rations with its noisy curtain hiding you from view.

A necklace of three more hills, what the geologists call Drumlins, lay to the west of Crookrise. In the centre, between the jaggedly cusped Skyraikes and the humped Sugarloaf, was Sharphaw. That is how it is spelt and I've only just found out, for it's always known as

'Sharper'. From Skipton it looks like a small volcano, conical and pointed. In reality it is a ridge like a house top, presenting the gable end to view. This we discovered when we scaled it, carrying tin trays on which we sledged exhilaratingly down again on the bracken.

I have spent much of my life surrounded by moor, fell and mountain. Rather more of it in fact than in the flatter environs of East Anglia. With a foot in each camp for as long as I can remember, I have learned to love them both. Yorkshire folk in my experience realize with something of a shock on return from holiday in Norfolk, say, or abroad in the Netherlands, that they have missed the hills. 'We had a grand time. Bye! but it's nice to get back to your own bed. And it was so flat!' The encircling hills draw the eye to the far horizon and the broad sweeps. Once over the hill and into the next dale, a new landscape lies below – a quick change of colour, of geology, of flora and fauna and quite frequently of weather. This has resulted in the individuality of the small towns and villages, and the change as you travel from rural market town to industrial mill town can be staggeringly rapid.

In Skipton you can almost draw a line across the road where one begins and the other finishes. Originally 'Sheep Town', the country character has been preserved by the stubborn attitude of the feudal families occupying the Castle, who refused to allow the canal and later the railway to encroach on the centre of the town. The reasons were commercial rather than aesthetic, but it had the effect of keeping the mills to the southern perimeter. It was quite different in nearby Keighley, Bingley and Bradford, where they burgeoned and blackened in the town centres.

The Raikes rise at the northern end of Skipton, and in my boyhood it was a short hop over a drystone wall into the fields and pasture. On most afternoons we would be captured, scrubbed and smartly clad to walk down into the town on shopping expeditions, Granny hatted and gloved with a capacious handbag. Granny was as tiny as Gramp was long and lean, which made him look oddly protective when they were walking together. Our route lay downhill past the forge and the old pinfold and a cemetery where we were told Rudyard Kipling's father was buried. Further down, a bridge crossed the old castle moat by Stanforth's Celebrated Pork Pie Establishment. We were never clear how you celebrated a pork pie, but felt it must have something to do with the huge stand pie which always arrived at Christmas as a present to valued customers.

Past the parish church, the wide High Street opened out, cobbled either side, without the columns of parked vehicles which hide its spacious breadth today. Opening on to the pavement at intervals between shops were narrow cobbled passages, or 'ginnels', known as 'The Yards'. Gramp told us that hundreds of years ago the townsfolk would barricade themselves inside the Yards when marauding Scots came sweeping through Skipton. 'The Emperor Hadrian built a wall,' he would say, 'from Firth of Forth to Forth of Clyde, to keep out the savage Picts and Scots. And still the beggars get through!' (I think it was 'beggars'.) On the setts stood the open market stalls – much more fun than the shops – and cattle and sheep were still driven down the High Street to the cattle market on Mondays and Wednesdays.

Progress was predictably slow, as my grandparents seemed to know everybody, and every few yards we had to stop and be introduced. 'Are these Sam's lads?' and of course the perennial 'Nay! Haven't they grown!' Our Skipton roots go back more than a century.

My grandfather's optician's shop was our ultimate goal on shopping afternoons, especially the cosy office-cum-workshop at the back, where there was a friendly fire in winter and I was allowed to make my first experimental forays on a sturdy typewriter.

The front of the shop was protected by a glazed Victorian canopy, relic of the large jeweller's, where it was important that customers could gaze into the windows and choose their hunters, fob-chains or engagement rings undaunted by wet weather. Sadly it has recently been pulled down. Two plate glass bays flanked the entrance where a smart slatted oak gate was padlocked at closing time. Gramp had a flair for advertisement, and in the window a stuffed long-eared owl, perched on a suspended crescent moon, peered out through a pair of gold-rimmed spectacles. There was even a macabre case of glass eyes, each balefully glaring upwards. On one occasion a large, lobed potato was dug up in the allotment, its shape unmistakably that of a seal, with raised head above two flippers and a tapering body. This duly went into the window, wearing a minute pair of glasses, fronted by a placard reading: 'Potatoes have many eyes; you have only two. Take care of them!'

Natural history was a family obsession, though in the Gilbert White, Izaak Walton fashion. We learned it all in a practical way, not academically. In this Gramp was a great mentor, as of course was my father, but I think grandparents have more time for you – and walk a bit more slowly. Granny was a sound authority on wild flowers.

Gramp's stories were marvellous – usually sparked off by the actual site where the event took place, so you knew they must be true. For instance, he would point to the Old Pound at the bottom of Castle Hill:

'There was a big funeral procession came past here from the Raikes when I was a lad. Hearse drawn by four black horses – polished silver and nodding black plumes – the mourning husband sitting up in front with the driver. They took that corner by the church wall a bit fast and the coffin slid away on to the road. The lid flew off and the old girl sat up and rubbed her eyes. Five years later she died again, and once again the procession came down from the Raikes. Just here the husband tapped the driver on the shoulder. "Go canny round next corner, lad!"'

His tales of the market stalls were colourful. There was, according to Gramp, the lurid character who sold 'a penn'orth o' liver and a suck of bacon'. He fried the liver and had a roll of toasted bacon on a string. You ate your liver and had a good chew and a swallow at the bacon. He then pulled it up and went on to the next customer. And the two old dears at the tripe and trotter stall:

'Nay, this tripe is stringy, Martha!'
'Try eating it with your veil up, love!'

I remember a typical occasion when we were fishing in the baby Wharfe among the limestone pools and fissures towards Langstroth-dale. 'D'ye see that farm?' said Gramp, pointing across the iron bridge at Yockenthwaite. 'In the old days, before farmers had cars, the traveller would come round in September, before the snows came, and the farmer's wife would stock up with everything she needed to see her over the winter – for he wouldn't be round again till the spring. To every farm he visited he would bring a present from his stock-in-trade. This particular year it was one of the new brushes for the privy, with a pink, celluloid handle. It was much admired. The following March, when the road was open, he called again, with enquiries as to how they had fared over the winter. "And how d'you get on with the little lavatory brush I gave you?" The farmer's wife was thoughtful. "Aye, it were very pretty and we all give it a try. But, I don't know – somehow we've gone back to paper."'

We adored our holidays in Skipton, and our attachment to the Yorkshire Dales became firmly rooted when, just after the war, our grandparents moved to a little gem of a cottage in Threshfield in Wharfedale. Home, however, was in Hertfordshire, and we were always glad to get back to our village and the butterfly nets.

2

Summer's Lease

Oak Eggar moth

IN CONTRAST TO SKIPTON, OUR KITCHEN AT HOME IN HERTFORDSHIRE was miniscule. A coke-hungry black range backed on to the big chimney which it shared with the ingle-nook next door in the lounge. A small table covered in American Cloth – the early 1940s equivalent of today's plastic, oily and squeaky to the touch and smelling of new paint – gave no scope for our (non-culinary) pursuits. Crammed in somehow, immigrant from London, was that indispensible piece of pre-war kitchen furniture, the Easiwork Cabinet. Its interior was designed to hold everything that a kitchen required except the cook; plates, knives, pans and jars fitting snugly into slots and clips like the galley on a small yacht fitted out to withstand rough weather. When, later, the local joiner managed to insert cupboards between the beams, tongued and grooved and stained dark oak, a rustic forerunner of the 'fitted kitchen', the cabinet was made over to us, to house all our entomological equipment.

American Cloth was not the only oily offering to the atmosphere. Firelighters were provided by porous bricks in wire cages which spent the day soaking up paraffin in a tray at the bottom of one of the cupboards. The beams and the two bare oak staircases were regularly polished with linseed oil. House mice and fieldmice would nightly queue up on the handrails to lick it off. Above the dining-room staircase, and a treacherous beam designed to stun the unwary, hung an oak cupboard where, early in the war, the morphine supply for the village and other first-aid paraphernalia were kept in case of air raids.

Another interesting cupboard, almost requiting our longing for the secret passage which surely must have lain somewhere in our Tudor cottage, was a little door inset at shoulder height into the wall of the landing. One could squeeze through this, as in a pot-hole, climb up the sloping bricks of the central chimney stack and gain access to the loft and the underdrawing of the roof. As the water tanks were housed up here and it was an extremely tight fit for a twentieth-century adult (Elizabethans were presumably much smaller; none of the doorways was much higher than five feet), a trap door was eventually built in the ceiling of the central bedroom, opening to an attic and a dormer window in the rear of the roof. Mr Carter, the joiner, erected what seemed an enormous ladder outside from the back garden. I made the perilous ascent once he had broken through, excited curiosity overcoming my fear of the height – which cannot have been more than twenty-five feet.

Derelict half-timbered cottages were not uncommon around us then, victims of neglect rather than enemy action, and materials and tiles of a suitable vintage, even leaded windows, were easily come by. Mr Carter found what appeared to be the initials of one of his ancestors carved into one of the old bricks, so we presumed his family had been the original builders of the cottage. Certainly they had been in the trade as long as anyone could remember. His father was a lean, vague old man, knobbled hand leaning on a stick, with a white fringe of beard like those worn by the smocked farm-hands of early photographs. Much lath and plaster was removed, and out of curiosity samples were taken to London for analysis. They proved to contain human hair and urine, which conjured up wildly intriguing pictures of early cement-mixing.

The past seeped from every beam. I would sit on the dining-room stairs – a dark, quiet spot for meditation – and idly wonder how many other boys had sat here and how they were dressed. There had been a door once, at the bottom, which must have been inconvenient. Who had drilled that neat hole in the oak? And if it had held a peg, what was it for? Here I would sit in my pyjamas and listen to *Saturday Night Theatre* from below until a chair creaked a warning and I would creep silently back to bed to avoid discovery until the coast was again clear. We were not welcome downstairs after lights-out. The rooms were subtly transformed at night. In the daytime they were our domain, but then they belonged to the grown-ups, strangely exciting, warm and smoky. One night Patrick ventured below, with the excuse that he was thirsty. Tim and I listened intently to see how this subterfuge paid off. He was, a little unsympathetically, offered a glass of water.

'I'm not thirsty for water,' complained our adventurer, 'I'm thirsty for cake!' This became a family aphorism. Anyone pursuing some devious intent was 'thirsty for cake'.

In the daytime our activities centred round 'The Hut'. This multi-purpose den, with its tones of Richmal Crompton, was built for us in the summer of 1940 at the top of the garden. Four square, of solid timber, gabled with two windows, it was our exclusive lair except for periodic swoops when matriarchal authority demanded that it be swept and garnished and generally tidied up. It contained all our toys and treasures, the demoted Easiwork cabinet, shabby furniture and all our collecting equipment. All expeditions started and finished here.

Many of our toys were home-made. We learned from friends of

our own age how to make whistles from hollowed elder twigs. A ten-inch section of ash branch could be drilled down the centre with a red-hot poker, to take a length of dowling. These were once used for giving pills to horses. Chewing up a paper pellet, squashing it in one end of the bore and ramming the rod down the other, produced a highly satisfactory and very noisy pop-gun. A naturally growing plaything was provided by the prevalent 'fools' barley', a persistent weed growing in any meagre patch of earth at the feet of walls or in the cracks between paving stones. The heads made streamlined missiles, but if you put one into your sleeve and worked your arm up and down it would crawl up to your shoulder. By skilful shrugging at this stage, we could make it cross at the back and work its way out again down the other sleeve.

Much of this (probably ancient) lore passed to us when Tim and I joined the Village School in 1941. This plunge into a new environment has been described so vividly by Laurie Lee in *Cider with Rosie* and, though ours was a different school and indeed a different decade, our experiences were so similar, that I hardly dare to follow him. Though I was not told to 'wait there for the present' (which never materialized), the friendly headmistress suggested that I should 'go and sit with the lambkins'. It sounded comfortably pastoral. Geoffrey Lambkin and his sister, also newcomers, were the evacuees of our butterflying Rector, and Geoffrey and I became friends and allies, sharing the same route home. This, the scenic route, crossed Mr Ritch's farm, burrowed through a tract of long grass and tangled bushes which we called the 'Jungle' and shot abruptly through a hedge into the High Street down a slide in the high, sandy bank. Not surprisingly, we were always a bit dusty when we got home.

At school I found to my hot shame that I was wearing girls' shoes. The Mill Boys came in old cord breeches and leather laced boots and were vociferous in their scorn. The offending footwear had narrow straps which buttoned across the instep. All parents must know the frustration of buying often expensive garments which their children won't wear because of social taboos which may sound trivial. In those days of rationing, this must have seemed even more unreasonable, but I refused, wildly tearful, in spite of protest and threat, ever to wear those shoes again.

The Mill Boys, who became staunch friends once my feet conformed to regulations, were a mixed bunch of orphans who were fostered at the old water-mill. John Cooper; Tommy Cullen . . . their roll sounded rather like the chorus of Widdicombe Fair. I saw little of them out of school. Once home, they were put to work. However, John was a liberal provider of tow, useful in my early essays in taxidermy. Where he got it from in such quantities I never found out, but I stuffed a partridge for him. He would also bring me the occasional Old Lady moth, a species which seemed to frequent the mill: big, square black moths with a Gothic tracery in pale ochre resembling an old-fashioned crochet shawl.

New school friends widened our knowledge of the local byways, and a few shared our interest in natural history. Wildlife had a certain untaught sanctity among us, though the general attitude was anything but conservationist. Wild things were there either to be shot as pests, shot for the pot or poached for profit. There was little deliberate cruelty; it was an attitude that had been handed down for centuries. Man was still just holding his own against nature, without the aid of chemical warfare to tilt the balance in favour of huge monocultures, protected at the expense of unsuspected links in food chains and of plants and of animals which, to be fair, were never the targets in the first place. The parable of the tares in the wheat has taken on a new significance. If the tares are suppressed entirely, the consequences reach beyond all telling, a danger to all of us.

Poaching for the pot seemed a mild enough branch of felony. We would nobble the wire snares that we often came across by slipping the noose free, but this was because we abhorred the thought of the strangled rabbit rather than any urge to champion authority. We would tickle trout in the little River Beane in the pebbly reaches, lying flat on the grassy bank above. 'Tickling' is a misleading description. You reach into the water under the bank and feel about gently. When you feel the presence of a fish, you start imperceptibly to stroke his tummy from head to tail (a trout always lies with his head upstream). He rather likes this, it lulls him into a restful coma, and your stroking fingers gradually curl and move forward, nearer to the gills. Finally you grip him behind the gills and fling him upwards with a jerk on to the bank. In practice it is not as easy as I have made it sound, and would-be young poachers will be far better served putting in a legitimate apprenticeship with rod and line, but it was a deliciously lazy pursuit on a sunny afternoon.

Frogs respond in a similar way. We would catch a frog and hold it gently on its back while it struggled. Stroking its tummy downwards with a wet finger had a hypnotic effect, and it would lie, comatose, while we examined it. Once turned the right way up again it would come to, with a 'What the hell am I doing here?' expression, and dive for freedom with a convulsive leap.

Scrumping in the apple orchards was a further escapade in our calendar of crime. Why the scrumping season always fell at a time when the apples were green, immature and acidly unpalatable I cannot guess, but so it was. There was something about the laden fruit trees which brought out the thieving instincts of the most law-abiding of us. Red Indian tactics were called for, scaling fences and wriggling through long grass. Such illicit harvesting would be prob-lematical today, but in those days shirts had tails. At a signal we would all stand up, fill our shirt fronts with as many apples as we could speedily grab, and bolt wildly for the fence, many a time to the accompaniment of pursuing shouts and curses. Over the fence, spilling fruit as we scrambled, we would split up and, by many devious routes, reassemble on the village green. We had apples enough of our own at home, but they never had the same flavour. Thus it ever was, and the grass is always greener, not to say the apples, in the next meadow. Repeated tummy-aches, more painful than any chastisement, failed to dim the lure. Maybe Eden's serpent has been maligned all these years. I don't think Eve needed any aid to temptation, she just put the blame on him afterwards.

I must digress, not that I am very good at sticking to the subject anyway, to tell you of an essay which my grandmother treasured over the years from her infant-teaching days. It was dated 1908, and a little girl was telling the story of the Fall of Man. The dénouement leaves one gasping. 'And God said to Eve, "Did you partake of that there apple?" And Eve said, "No God." And God said to Adam, "Did you partake of that there apple?" And Adam said, "No God." And God said, *"Then what about them two cores?"* '

At times moth and caterpillar collecting would be a social activity when word got round that any particular area was favourable. In late July, as the cornfields were being cut, Oak Eggar moths were reported at Moss Bury. The large, furry males fly frantically about searching for the larger, even furrier females, who sit down sensibly and wait for them. Our quarry was the male, and a dozen or so of us spent exhausting afternoons chasing these swift, powerful fliers, chocolate brown in the sunshine, round stook and stack, making wild swipes with the nets as we ran. Mothing was a passing fancy for most of our friends, and fickle caprice would pass on to ferreting on the common, or combing the potato fields for Colorado beetles in the hope of the advertised reward. Only we three with one or two companions remained steadily faithful to the moths and butterflies.

The cornfields were enclosed by tall hedges, providing cover and long zig-zag cross-country routes where there were no official footpaths. Rabbits used to crop the young wheat and barley a yard or so from the hedge bottom, so we could walk along the hedges without fear of treading on the corn. The destruction of mile after mile of hedges, to extend the fields into more 'viable' units, has resulted in an enormous loss of habitat for creatures which had lived there ever since the common land was enclosed. It is supreme irony that 'viable' means 'able for life to be carried on'.

The farmer is not today's Mr Hyde, changed from the Dr Jekyll of yesterday. He has always had to be eminently practical to survive at all. It is the scale of change that has endangered so much of our indigenous wildlife. Fields used to be small and hedged because small fields were the most economical way of diversifying crops and the hedges were the cheapest way of separating one from another. The ecological aspect never came into it. Admittedly many of the old-timers whom we knew as children were closer to the earth than a mere job would have warranted. They took an inordinate pride in a straight furrow (as though a crooked one wouldn't have served just as well) and would lift the harrow to avoid a tewit's nest, where today's lad in his enclosed tractor, transistor warding off boredom, may not know a corncrake from a cormorant.

It is not sentiment, certainly not sentimentality, which will save our natural heritage from eventual extinction. Only when it is realized by all that it is expedient, and in the long term practical common sense, to preserve the natural balance, will the perilous in-fighting among agriculture, development, industry and anxious naturalists give way to compromise and relative peace. We must ensure that such a day is not too far off, before, like the fabled scorpion, we also perish from our own poison.

Forty-five years ago there was little sign of dwindling population in the flora and fauna around us. Birds in their hundreds nested in field and bank, and insect life was prolific. Grasshoppers provided a ceaseless orchestra in the background when the sun shone. Should it disappear behind a cloud, the silence hit you like a sudden blow. Vain attempts to locate an individual instrumentalist by the sound attested to his extraordinary skill in ventriloquism. When a grass-hopper was released from the hand, the recoil from the punching hind legs was astonishingly powerful. Even the little froghoppers, whose soft, yellow nymphs had lived in their protective bubble baths of the pervasive 'cuckoo spit', gave an appreciable kick as they jumped off you.

Vulnerably fluttering, pale green lacewings abounded, with their metallic golden eyes, and we would bring them home to be released in the garden, for their larvae are voracious munchers of greenfly on the roses or blackfly on the broad beans. The little hover-flies which look like wasps are also gardeners' friends for the same reason, and we grew flowers among the vegetables to entice them in. Squat 'Miss Muffet' spiders, their domed bodies showing a range of colour and markings from emerald green to cream and dark chocolate, lurked patiently on the grasses and defied our attempts at identification. Along with beetles, infinitely varied in colour, shape and size, they were too numerous for specialist attention in addition to butterflies and moths. There had to be a limit, though 'Colyoptera' was a word that rolled pleasantly off the tongue. I once 'set' an earwig, teasing out the flimsy wings from under their tiny chitinous cases. However did they manage to fold them away again? The wings were in the perfect shape of a human ear, and of course the name is a corruption of 'Earwing'.

This gave us pause for thought. It wasn't the professors who gave things their country names, but the country people. They must have been far more observant than their twentieth-century counterparts. Plants with names such as coltsfoot and hare's ear, fleabane and self-heal, all give witness to scrutiny and medicinal knowledge handed down no doubt over centuries, now either lost, forgotten or ignored. One eccentric old necromancer of our acquaintance, who sported a venerable black homberg on his head and a faded brocade waistcoat across an expanse of tummy, could successfully 'charm' away warts, using the juice of the evening primrose which he would collect in small phials at a certain season. I found recently, on taking our Sealyham to the vet for treatment of a persistent allergy, that the evening primrose is once again being valued for its healing proper-ties. And very expensive it is too!

Among the grasshoppers we would occasionally find huge wing-less crickets, all of two inches in length: the climbing locust. Long-horned and stumpy, they were never common and seemed to be confined to a few banks in the farmland to the west of the village. We had house crickets at home in the brickwork round the ingle-nook who would give long high-pitched chirps when the fire was really hot. Chirps of contentment, not of complaint. They were even more plentiful in the bakery next door, for they revel in heat, to the extent that they would climb into the oven, and on two occasions we even found a cricket baked into the bread. It was probably suffocation rather than the heat that killed them.

Apart from the prevalent garden snails at which our garden song-thrush would hammer noisily away every morning with angry energy (we thought it must give him a headache), there must have been a score of different land species of snail in the countryside around us, of all colours and whorled, bulls-eye patterns. Prize among the shells, and sometimes found alive, was the huge edible snail, known locally as a Roman snail. Another folk memory, possibly, for the Romans were reputed to have brought them over from the Continent to breed as a delicacy. These were normally brown, brindled with dark red streaks, but those found on the chalk were uniformly white.

Patrick, ever alert to adapt a new pursuit, organized snail races: not, you may imagine, the most heart-stopping of competitive sports, but the results were surprising. The event lacked the urgency of the Derby but certainly lasted longer. Far from being on the flat, his galloping gasteropods raced over the sticks. Each had its own walled channel on the improvised track, and the hurdles were old razor blades. A snail can climb over a razor blade with impunity, its slime providing protection from damage. A lettuce leaf would be placed beyond the finishing post – and they were off! Fast favourites and 'good strait'uns' soon proved themselves. Racing snails would be marked with paint for identification and released in the garden, whence they could be rounded up and corralled for the next meeting.

The snails were left to roam where they could do little damage, in a secluded corner of the vegetable garden known, appropriately, as the 'Unpleasance'. Here, behind a screen of hedge, the incinerator flanked the compost heap, and groundsel and mayweed thrived on a mulch of cinders, old boots, decayed garden tools and broken flower pots. Every garden has its unpleasance. Such middens had extended to the surrounding countryside, wherever a bomb had left a crater in the fields defying subsequent ploughing or cultivation. Ever curious, we would sort through old bedsteads, split sofas and banks of corroded dry batteries for 'anything that might come in useful'.

It struck me that there was an infinitely depressing aura about man's decaying artifacts. Skeletons of bird and animal, dead trees and rotting carcases were unpleasant in themselves, but these had a rightness which mouldering car seats and rusty bed springs lacked. I suppose I had an instinctive feeling for the 'bio-degradable' (what an appalling word!) though we were not then swamped with today's seas of dismayingly indestructible plastic and polythene.

Searches in the craters were no more than idle diversions, accidental pauses in a ramble. Usually we would follow the lines of hedges to copse and spinney and eventually to the larger woods. Tree trunks, especially oak trees with their deep, creviced bark, are rich hunting grounds for moths. High Wood to the south of us had much oak and many sunny clearings. An expedition would require an early start, as the best time to find moths at rest is in the morning. Creatures of the dark, they tend to crawl deeper into niche or undergrowth when the sun gets high, but the morning finds them more exposed, where they have settled after the night's activity.

The aptly named Merveille du Jour is a conspicuously pretty moth, the forewings a pale lime green etched with crescent black markings edged with white. Seeing it in the display cabinet, you would doubt that it could be concealed anywhere. Only careful search would find them on the High Wood oak trees, where they would sit almost invisibly in the late summer. We soon found that a mothless tree trunk was the exception rather than the rule, though the real prizes were of course scarce.

Woodland is full of minor discomforts. Apart from brambly undergrowth away from the tracks and rides, the ground is usually moist and often treacherous. Mounds of sticky yellow clay were brought to the surface by the moles. We would bring it home for modelling and subsequent firing in the garden bonfire. Results would invariably be broken and crumbly. Well versed in the Scriptures, we remembered that you can't make bricks without straw. However, even this ingredient never seemed to help much, and besides it stuck out every which way and made a sculpted hippo look more like a hedgehog.

Small looper caterpillars would 'abseil' down from the thicket on gossamer threads which combined with the spiders' interlacing webs to spread stickily on your face. Holding the butterfly net in front of your nose avoided this nuisance, but then the net was vulnerable to thorn or bramble. Moving in single file, it was helpful to let one of the others take the lead, but this incurred the danger of a sudden swipe from a branch springing back from the path of the one in front. On our return the little loopers would have climbed half-way back, dangling free, taking in their safety lines as they mounted. We imagined their annoyance as, like Sysiphus, they plunged down again when we disturbed them for the second time.

Forays through High Wood would inevitably lead to the nearby village of Benington and lemonade at the back door of 'The Bell'. Sometimes, when accompanied by Dad at the weekend, we were privileged to go in at the front door. The landlord was a genial ex-pugilist with a cauliflower ear, a huge inflorescence which drew the eye in wonder. This fascination was enhanced by a splendid portrait of him, warts and all, which hung in the timbered bar parlour. This produced a weird doppelgänger effect and had me mechanically moving my gaze from one to the other and back like the devotees at Wimbledon.

A few years later a patch of plaster fell off the wall in the bar, above the fireplace, revealing a painting of a stag's head. Experts were (happily) called in and an entire Elizabethan stag hunt was laid bare under the plaster, complete save where it had extended over the ceiling beams and perished. I imagine it is still there.

The inhabitants of Benington liked to think that the name derived from the benign nature of the villagers, but it was more likely to have stemmed from the same root as the River Beane, which trickled on to them after leaving us. Though a charming little backwater, the village had once had its day. The King of Mercia had his palace here – King Bertulfe, or Berthulf, or Bert somebody anyway. That was in the far-off days when all our kings had names like Dogbreath or Eggfroth and were always having trouble with the Danes. In fact, in 850 or thereabouts King Bertulfe summoned a Great Council here in his palace and set off with his warriors towards London to do something about it. Unfortunately they were badly thrashed and the King died soon afterwards of disappointment.

We would usually follow the river back on the way home. In times of drought we could walk along the river bed, as it regularly dried up entirely.

Our own garden often yielded its own moths and caterpillars, and the hawthorn hedge provided two members of the family of Tussock moths. The family gets its name from the caterpillars which are all brightly patterned and extravagantly ornamented with tufts of coloured hair. One of the two in our garden was the Vapourer caterpillar, about an inch in length when full grown. A pale violet-grey over all, with red and yellow lines and spots, it has four deep yellow tussocks like shaving brushes rising from the back. The male Vapourer moth is a bright chestnut brown, an inch or so in wingspan. He flies incredibly quickly, vertically up and down the hedges, and is very hard to catch. Whenever one hatched out in the breeding cage he needed to be found early, as once dried out he might batter his wings to bits in his frantic flight. His lady is wingless. That is to say the wings are mere vestiges and of no use to her. This meant that the discovery of one caterpillar led to several more, as the female lays all her eggs within a small area, crawling from twig to twig.

In contrast the female of the other resident, the Gold Tail moth, is considerably larger than the male, with fluffy satin white wings spanning an inch and a quarter. The male is about two-thirds her size. Sitting on a leaf or a fence post, the moth looks like a downy white feather and as such must be frequently overlooked by collector and predatory bird. When disturbed it raises its body to display a hidden tail tipped by a tuft of golden yellow hairs. This is a warning signal to enemies, and for a particularly interesting reason. The caterpillars are easily found, for they make no effort to hide. Although they don't sport the lavish tussocks of the rest of the family, being content with a mere hump, they wear a conspicuous uniform of black with rows of vermilion and white patches along its length. Down the sides sprout stiff black and grey hairs. These hairs break off easily, and handling the caterpillar can result in an unpleasant nettle rash. Birds will avoid the larvae for this reason. What makes the Gold Tail unusual is that the protection is carried throughout the life cycle. The mature caterpillar spins a cocoon incorporating all the poisonous hairs. When a female hatches out, she spends quite a long time brushing her gold tail over the vacated cocoon. She lays her eggs in batches and leaves a fluffy patch of her gold tail with the protective hairs on each batch. She also has enough left to guard herself. The male doesn't arm himself like his mate, but his tail is the same colour and he presumably relies on her reputation to warn off predators.

The disadvantage of collecting in our own patch was that if we were seen or heard around, jobs would inevitably be found for us. Collared in this way, I once found the task had an unexpected bonus. I was raking in a seed-bed by a sallow tree, matured from a bean stick which had taken root and had been stuck into the hedge by the Unpleasance, when I turned up the large black chrysalis of a Poplar Hawk moth. Ever after that I would rake assiduously in the area, often quite unnecessarily, whenever the chance arose.

In 1940, before we were old enough to wander abroad, we had been encouraged to help with the task of dusting the newly heeled-in cabbages with a ring of Derris, shaking the powder from a muslin bag. Left to ourselves after the gardening week-end, we thought to polish our haloes by continuing the good work. Every possible growing thing was accordingly dusted. Regrettably, one sack of dust in the garage looked much like another, and the powder we had distributed so liberally was the compound used to rot down the compost heap. Impassioned and painful were the recriminations, and we determined to renounce voluntary good works for ever after.

Shortly after this a redoubtable old worthy was employed as a gardener – whether to assist the current digging for victory or to frustrate further helpful experiments from the junior ranks, we couldn't decide. We were never sure that our merits were truly appreciated. Dad would introduce us, in a row, as 'Pigsby, Dogsby and Little Bloody'. Old Charlie was wary of us to begin with, and we treated him with a cautious respect, which grew over the years to something near to affection. He was an infallible weather prophet. Most old countrymen claim to be, but he, a true Delphic, wisely backed it each way. 'I don't doubt but what it won't rain before night,' he'd say, scanning the sky shrewdly with tortoise eyes. After it had poured down all afternoon, Charlie would say with satisfaction, 'I said I didn't doubt but what it wouldn't rain before night.' On the other hand, after a fine, obstinately sunny day, he would say with equal assurance, 'I said I didn't doubt but what it *wouldn't* rain before night.'!

Charlie chewed a pungent brand of twist and was a champion spitter. We envied his deadly accuracy. A smouldering cigarette butt or the robin impudently eyeing him from beyond his delving fork – ping! – both were dealt with summarily. The habit was still rife among the local gaffers, though spittoons and sawdust had left the pubs. I was curious as to why the notices on the buses threatened a penalty of five pounds for spitting, whereas on the tube trains it was a mere two-pound fine, for thus it was. Perhaps, I reflected, they had more spitters on the Underground and could afford a reduction for numbers.

In later years the village instituted a pumpkin competition. It took on many of the characteristics of guerrilla warfare. Rival pumpkin growers would creep about peering through hedges and over garden fences to size up the opposition, and nobbling was not unheard-of. Charlie, I was delighted to learn, had lost none of his talent. His own monster, carefully hidden, was threatened only by the even more gargantuan growth of a simple lad of tender years who should never have been allowed to risk his life in such company. Charlie was generous with kindly advice. 'Look at them leaves!' said Charlie. 'Her'll never grow with all them leaves. Stands to reason! All the goodness is going into them leaves!' The lad duly sheared the leaves off, and Charlie reigned supreme.

Life moved on, immutably, and the seasons followed each other for four years while the war brought its alarms and adventures. The school leaving age was fourteen, and our little school ran the gamut from five. A handful of boys went at twelve to the grammar school at Stevenage and girls to the high school at Hitchin, but the majority stayed the final year and then left for the farms, or for shops, garages and the growing factories. Though well versed in the three 'r's and with, at ten, a knowledge beyond my years of literature, poetry and the natural world, I knew I would sometime have to add Latin, Greek and French to the menu, for I had often been told so.

The advent of the rocket bombs forced the final decision. In 1944 we learned that in September we were to be packed off to Yorkshire to prep school. That summer was one of farewells as each familiar moth and butterfly made its seasonal appearance and left the stage, and our free and easy life, far removed from cinema and dance hall and busy urban bustle, came to a close, never to revive with the same crisp intensity again.

3

Lusisti Satis

Peppered moths

Y OU'VE HAD ENOUGH FUN; TIME YOU WERE OFF!' THUS SPAKE
Horace in 68 BC – only he said it in Latin. The three Birdsall boys got
the same sort of message in 1944, some two thousand years later.
Doubtless a couple of millennia hence, should our suicidal old planet
survive, the stern refrain will still be sung and some dewy youth will
hear that his days of philandering are over.

The last precious week of freedom that September was spent in
Skipton. New clothes, results of hours of shopping and borrowed
coupons, had been amassed and lay in neat, unfamiliar piles in a
spare bedroom, together with three trunks, three handcases, all
boldly labelled with our names in black paint, and, supreme talisman
of the boarding school, a stout wooden 'tuck-box', corners reinforced with iron and fitted with a padlock, which we were to share.
All the clothes had been tried on and fitted. There were uncomfortable woolly vests and underpants. In our innocence we had survived
the war so far without pants, and vests had been mostly adult cast-
offs. Grey flannels were not insisted on, owing to clothes rationing,
but grey shirts were mandatory. The school tie was no longer
available, another rationing casualty, and we had substitutes of a
plain bright red, incongruously left-wing for neophytes entering into
'privileged' education. Neither the political irony nor the privilege
struck us with any force at the time.

The womenfolk seemed to spend their days in a permanent
'sewing bee', attaching the indispensible Cash's name tapes to every
article in the entire trousseau. Shoes all required a name and
number. My number was 10. Black outdoor shoes, elastic-sided
house shoes, gym shoes, bedroom slippers, rugger boots, gumboots –
it looked as though we were going to spend considerable time each
day slotting feet from one form of footwear into another. I saw with a
pang that a lifetime of regimentation stretched ahead of me, too far
to comprehend but desolately infinite.

Dad had taken a rare holiday on this occasion – the only time I can
recall during the entire war – and entered into a tacit agreement with
us that the coming wrench was never going to take place. As I came
to realize later, such upheavals, ranking with weddings, births and
funerals, are largely the concern of the women of the family, who
call on mysterious reserves of ancestral skill and secret wisdom. The
four of us kept out of the way, and spent our time fishing or in long
walks over the familiar moors, on one occasion asserting our
presence by arriving back to a thorough scolding for being cold and
wet through. We were rubbed and dried and placed shamefacedly

around the kitchen fire with our feet in hot mustard baths – a preventive therapy which seems to have disappeared along with bread poultices.

The eve of departure was marked by a party and our customary pieces and recitations. In our house Tim had devised an ever popular hit by bowdlerizing a rhyme learnt from his village schoolfellows. The substitution of a single consonant had spruced up this offering for polite company, an epic involving a Mr Brown who went to town and 'threw a dart' behind a cart and paralysed the pony. I was always acutely embarrassed as Tim wound through the fable with studiedly feigned innocence. Neither of us realized that the audience was usually as *au fait* with the original as we were and relished the complicated situation. As Patrick finished his repertoire of nursery rhymes – he was six and a half by this time – Gramp admonished the company to remember the occasion, as never would they hear the same artless performances again. Like Wordsworth, he knew that the shades of the prison house would soon begin to close.

We were not due at Malsis Hall until late afternoon, so the day started with a final tramp with Dad on the moor. Fate was rubbing it in a bit, for we found a colony of Fox moth caterpillars. I recalled with a pang that I must leave these beauties at liberty, for I did not know whether the future would hold any provision for looking after them. We arrived home for lunch rather late, for feet were inclined to drag, and changed out of corduroy breeches and boots and favourite, shabby jackets. Then baths and into our new gear feeling already that the old life was fast vanishing. I understood then that individuality was something I wanted fiercely to retain. Into my new suitcase I surreptitiously smuggled my folding butterfly net.

So we were plunged into a sea of new faces, strange customs and the time-honoured catechism of 'What's-your-name-where-d'ye-come-from-what's-your-father-do?' Each new boy had a guardian angel of around his own age appointed to look after him. Officially, newcomers were allowed a fortnight's grace to get used to the regime and discipline, after which they took their chance with authority like everyone else. The fifteenth day was known with eloquent simplicity by our seasoned fellows as the 'Newbugs' Bashing Day'.

The cloistered, though hardly quiet, character of such an enclosed little community as a preparatory school in the 1940s had probably changed little since the previous century. Comfort was considered unmanly but good manners were obligatory. I have always been delighted by the charming story that Queen Victoria never looked behind her when sitting down; she would seat herself wherever the fancy took her, confident in the knowledge that a chair would be swiftly placed in a position to avert disaster. Miss Lee, diminutive doyenne of the English department, could walk with prim authority and a daunting pile of books from one end of the school to the other without pause, never having to open a door. Admittedly she risked violent upset from the half-dozen boys rushing at each threshold to open it for her. Were members of staff met on the wide, imposing staircase, we would fling ourselves, quite unnecessarily as there was room for a coach and horses, flat against the wall until they had passed.

One of the masters surprised me as I was adding a moth to the 'relaxing tin', a container which kept specimens in a pliable state until they could be transferred to the setting board. I think he suspected it was a tin of sweets I had secreted in my locker. He was rather impressed. I had found some melanistic specimens of the Peppered moth. To explain, in the south the moth takes its name from its pepper and salt specks sprinkled on a pale grey background. Every so often it produces a variety which is uniformly black. This is a common enough phenomenon in many animals, and is known as 'melanism'. Against a tree trunk the pale moth is effectively camouflaged, whereas the black ones will show up and be speedily picked off by predatory birds. In industrial Yorkshire in those days (we were on the frontier of the mills) the trees and buildings were more or less black. This environment reversed the trick and the dark moths were the preponderant ones.

A favourite of mine among Tim's large cartoon drawings, published in *The Spectator* in the early sixties, depicts a pair of prosperous business men making for the old Leeds City Station against a background of stygian smoke, belching chimneys and dark, satanic mills. 'Smokeless Zone?' one is saying, 'Nay, lad, tha can't tamper wi' Nature!' Since then the decline in textiles has combined with the sand blaster and anti-pollution legislation, and the buildings no longer loom obscurely out of veils of black smog. I have not yet discovered whether this has made any appreciable difference to the appearance of the Peppered Moths.

Few mill chimneys were in sight. The moors stretched southwards uninterrupted to the Brontës' Haworth. The house itself was fairly typical of the mansions built in the middle of the last century by the local wool barons. At the top of the drive, about a quarter of a mile of it, cobbled on the steep parts to prevent the horses slipping in cold weather, a sturdy porch guarded the front door. A square stone canopy extended from the frontage, supported by heavy Palladian pillars, housing on their plinths a pair of draughtily clad young ladies representing spring and autumn. They carried appropriate stone fruit to justify their respective titles. The massive oak door, carved with lions' heads, was opened with a sturdy click by a proportionately huge brass knob. This you pushed to gain entrance, to the chagrin of many visitors who would waste vain minutes turning it to no avail.

The door swung weightily open to glazed doors, intricately engraved with frosted urns, more lions and heraldic birds, which in turn pushed open into the hall. A square well opened above to the height of the house, surrounded by a gallery, ideal site for angel choirs during the carol services, giving a sense of airy space. This was later covered to support an extra dormitory, practical and necessary, but the lofty effect was destroyed.

Fireplaces were ornate; cold white marble nymphs and caryatids, or dark black and green veined blocks of solidity surmounted by mahogany and mirrors. All the classrooms had coal fires, screened by capacious wire fireguards, their panels moulded into boy-shaped recesses, testaments to generations of back-warming. These were augmented by an ancient labyrinth of massive iron central heating pipes which echoed like stethoscopes to any disturbance and rumbled internally, a vast intestinal system. Sitting on the 'fug-pipes' was a coveted luxury and subject to a strict pecking order.

Two enclosed narrow flights of steep, dark wooden stairs, the servants' backstairs in the house's heyday, led from the dormitories to the back passage below. An old 'blowpipe', predating the house telephone, still communicated between the floors. One could carry on conversations very effectively through this system until discovered and summarily turfed off. The passage led to the back door, past the butler's pantry and the housekeeper's parlour, in our time the masters' and ladies' common rooms respectively. A strange marvel occurred in the back passage, paved as it was in a pattern of octagonal tiles in contrasting colours. The eyes would 'lock' on to the pattern deceptively, giving the impression of wading knee deep in the floor. Rows of numbered pegs flanked the passage, hung with macs and coats, and it was here that we used to assemble for walks in wet weather, along with Rusty, an elderly (and usually wet) golden cocker spaniel. 'School Dog' was as traditional as 'Ship's Cat', and we were nothing if not traditionalists. Sterile nylon anoraks and waxed thornproofs have rendered extinct the reek of wet rubber macintoshes; it is a (not unpleasant) flavour which pervaded most of my schooldays.

Mornings started with the cold plunge – one of the privileges I would willingly have foregone. Many stalwarts swore they enjoyed it and even claimed it warmed them up, crowing over the reluctance of an effete southerner. Reluctant or no, at the summons of the bell at half-past-seven we all trooped downstairs in our dressing-gowns to the plunge bath provided by the erstwhile wool magnate who in his day, the sybarite, had had it heated. In winter the plunge continued daily until a cough or cold absolved you. I remained agonizedly healthy for week after week. Those completing the term won the then grand reward of half-a-crown. Needless to say my first serious sniffle would invariably manifest itself with little more than a fortnight to go.

Admittedly the ordeal left one warmer and wide awake, but Sparta was not done with us yet. Once dressed, it was down to the bootroom, leaving beds nakedly stripped, and out down the drive before breakfast. The custom was to bring back a certifying leaf from a poplar tree which grew by the front gate. It was the only one among countless elms, beech, sycamore and ash trees which lined the drive above a thicket of rhododendron. Certain Athenians laid in a store of leaves to enable them to curtail the daily trip, but sudden *appels* would be organized sporadically when a prefect would be waiting at the bottom of the drive with a roll-call.

The ornate cast-iron gates were supported by heavy stone pillars, one either side. The Lancashire border was some three miles up the road to the south-west. This famous road 'over t'Moss' was, by Yorkshire consent, the only good thing to come out of Lancashire. Thus adherents of the white rose would touch the left-hand gate post on reaching the bottom, while those of the County Palatine would touch the right. I classed myself among the handful of off-comed'uns from the south who performed a dignified about-turn bang in the centre. Years later gates and posts were removed for a time while the West Riding Council widened the road. When they were replaced, the posts were put back the wrong way round. With supreme schoolboy logic the relative touching stations were reversed, succeeding generations conforming but not really understanding why they did.

At the entrance to the dining-room stood a large ebony elephant. This too was touched by long custom by every boy on his way in and on his way out. As progress was in single file, a bottleneck frequently occurred when a boy clawed his way back against the stream with, when upbraided, the perfectly reasonable explanation that he had 'forgotten to touch the elephant'. Mealtimes were somewhat cramped compared with home. You learnt to eat with elbows clamped to the ribs. Sitting in strict 'form order', we moved clockwise round our particular tables one place daily, so at intervals would fetch up sitting next to a member of staff at one or other end. This involved the menial business of serving and clearing away and invariably sycophantic conversation: 'Ooh, Sir! Gosh, Sir! That's a spiffing tie, Sir!'

Domestic staff were in short supply; most of the girls were Irish and presumably not drafted into war work. As I grew older it occurred to me what a paradox it was that comfortable, middle-aged ladies in the kitchen were known as 'maids', while the prattling ingénues in the upstairs regions were called 'matrons'. Chores such as washing-up in kitchen and pantry and spud bashing were shared by the boys on a rota basis – just like home. Hefty columns of dinner plates were clasped against the chest and dried by wiping the top and bottom ends of the pile, then sliding the top plate underneath. This was considered quicker than drying each plate separately. An arguable theory which in practice left a sopping shirt front to add to the discomfort of plunging hands into revolting cold porridge pans to scour out the glutinous dross from their depths. In the dining-room the tables were cleared and swabbed, and an unhealthily sweet-smelling viscous pink polish was flicked from a tin with a stick on to their surface, to be rubbed in and energetically buffed until they shone.

The toast rota proclaimed another chore. The toasters, three in number, rose at six-thirty and set to work on carefully counted piles of doorsteps (one per boy was the ration) in a big, gas fuelled grill. Bakers hadn't hit on the idea of selling sliced bread in those days, and the job was done for us the night before with a wicked-looking bacon slicer which was strictly off limits. You made sure that you supplied your own table last of all, and marched importantly into the dining-room as breakfast started, bearing a tray of fresh hot toast for your mates and an extra slice for yourself, like a boar's head at a medieval banquet.

Breakfast over, we all climbed the stairs back to the dormitories for the mysteries of bed-making and hospital corners. Beds had a welcome individuality as you had your own rug. Mine was a

Campbell tartan. I was a poor bed-maker. Results were all inspected before the dormitory was permitted to depart, and too often my fellows would shift impatiently while my efforts were pulled to bits and meticulously reassembled. I failed to appreciate the logic behind it. After all, I was the one destined to sleep in it, and if I didn't mind the odd wrinkle, why should anyone else? Free at last, we would scamper downstairs to bury noses into 'gender rhymes' and 'principal parts', the daily offering from 'Kennedy's Shortbread Eating Primer', to be kenned by rote before morning prayers.

As Latin has become more or less optional at even our oldest universities, let alone prep schools, some explanation is no doubt necessary. With a few deft strokes of the pen, LATIN can be transformed into EATING, a perennial joke which has graced textbooks down the ages. I remember a *Punch* cartoon of a bill poster in the Underground, sticking up advertisements showing ladies with flourishing facial hair and heavy spectacles, and explaining, '. . . so now we print them with the moustaches already on'. Whether the weary Ritchie eventually published his work as 'FIRST STEPS IN EATING', I cannot recollect, but he might just as well have done. It is unlikely that the poet Livy ever dreamt that he would be immortalized in the memories of generations of reluctant classical scholars for his 'SLIMY LEGENDS OF ANCIENT ROME'.

Sundays brought a respite from Latin verbs and even an extra hour in bed in the morning. Sunday breakfast was, even in wartime, invariably eggs. Eggs solidly annealed and toughened in commodious wire baskets – none of your lightly boiled please and I prefer a brown one – which spread sulphurous fumes as seventy of these dainties were noisily decapitated in staccato unison. Before choir practice there was the compulsory sabbath ritual of 'Letter-writing Prep'.

Considering the amount of writing which filled our time during the week, it is strange to reflect on the hardship involved in racking the brain for something to say when writing home. It seemed an impossible contortion to relate the imminent reality of school life to the distant dream world of home comforts and family unity. As a result, letters, even from the most articulate, tended to be stereotyped and perfunctory. A letter home from Tim is typical of the sort of thing:

Friday 25–5–45

Dear Mummy and Daddy,

Thankyou for the postcard of Trafalgar Square. Do you think you could send me a bottle of Lemonade Crystals? Most of the boys here have got them, and they are very nice. Half Term is on June 9th. We have had a play and I was a ghost. I am 3rd in Latin, 14th in French, 5th in English and 10th in Form Order. I am getting on quite well and am looking forwards to Sports Day.

All my love,

Tim

I forget which ghost Tim was referring to. I spent an inordinate time writing plays, producing plays and performing plays, from satirical romps in camera to amuse the immediate company after lights-out, to more dignified drama in public. My parents worried that I might be wasting too much time on such fruitless fantasy (the stage was still not considered quite respectable) but Bernard Gadney, the headmaster, advised them to let me get it out of my system. It reminds me of the lovely old Chelsea Pensioner sitting with his mate on a park bench and reflectively eyeing the pretty girls passing by.

'D'ye remember that stuff they used to give us in trenches to stop us thinkin' about women?'

'Aye, bromide, what of it?'

'I think 'appen mine's beginning to work!'

I still haven't really got it out of my system, and fear I never shall.

Early in 1945 I contracted osteomyelitis in the joints of my right index finger. Luckily for me, penicillin, though in its infancy, was now available. I stress the locality of the infection for I often reflect that without the new drug, had I survived (no certain outcome, for the disease was then a killer) I would have suffered at worst an amputation, at best a finger which had ceased to grow at the age of ten. Drawing and painting, playing the oboe – even writing – all the activities which have meant so much to me in life, would have been problematical to say the least.

The clinical trials of penicillin had advanced with urgent priority owing to the war. Supply, however, was limited and the bulk was going out to the troops, many at that time fighting the 'Battle of the Bulge' in the Ardennes. I remember this particularly, as I was fighting my own 'Battle of the Bulge', my hand having swollen to grotesque size under its bandages, about as useful as a boxing glove. There was no penicillin immediately available in Leeds and Bradford. At that time it could be kept in a refrigerator only for three or four days. Here again fortune favoured me. My father, a senior consultant and a personal friend of the Floreys, was able to drive up from London twice a week with precious supplies of the drug in an insulated canister, supplies which, I am pleased to say, came to the aid of other patients beside myself.

I was one of the first civilians in the West Riding to be saved by penicillin. I suffered injections in my beam end, day and night, every ninety minutes for the first week. Sleeplessness was the most worrying side-effect for early patients. When the intervals were extended to three hours it seemed a luxury. Cheerful nurses would assure me that in a year or so the treatment would be given in tablets – scant comfort to me at the time. Prompted by a serial on the wireless, precocious infant, I spent the first painful week reading *Barlasch of the Guard*.

A letter written to me at the time has survived the years. It was from Bernard Gadney, more famed for his prowess on the rugby field than on the typewriter. The very letterhead is a time capsule from days when telephones and cars were sparse but other forms of transport more extensive. (Reproduced on opposite page.)

My eventual convalescence in the summer term debarred me from cricket practice. I spent many afternoons with the butterfly net. A charming little black moth with narrow white edges, the Chimney Sweeper, flew in the hayfields which had replaced many of the school playing fields during the war. I rarely spot one nowadays, but then most of the grass is cut green for silage and hay is a rare commodity. The cricket was presided over by Mr Harold Phillips, a dear old man who taught us History and Latin. He had served with distinction in the Boer War, and spent the twilight of his life painstakingly coaching generations of small boys in the game he loved and lavishing skill and affection on a square of emerald turf, the envy of most schools and clubs in the Riding.

I missed out on his early coaching, and I never showed much prowess at cricket. However, I am left-handed with anything requiring two hands, such as wielding a broom, an axe or a cricket bat, and although I was never at the wicket long, I used to savour the sense of power as fielders twigged and ran to change sides, and, especially, when the square-leg umpire asked diffidently if he could stay put.

From *The Headmaster*,
Malsis Hall, Cross Hills, Near Keighley, Yorkshire.
Telephone and Telegrams—Cross Hills 91.   Station—Kildwick L.M.S.
Bus Stop—Dog & Gun Inn, on route Keighley—Colne

11th February 1945.

My dear James,

    I am really showing off a bit sending you
a typed letter !   It would look more interesting
if you were here to give the keys a big clop with
your flipper.   I am so pleased you are keeping
cheery and may (you see I made a mess of the and !)
you be back with us soon.   It looks as though
you will have to wade through the snow.   Reggie is
in bed still with his cough.   I hope to get in to
see you again soon.   Take care of yourself. All
the best old boy,   Love from us all,   *[signature]*

If this was a business letter I should put at the
bottom.

James Birdsall Esq.,
Room. 3. Duke of York's Home,
Bradford.

one day when I am an old man and you are famous I
expect I shall have to write:-
Sir James Birdsall Bart.,
    1. Harley Street,   or do you want to be the
        London. W. 1.   other end of the street ? !

It's rather like tasting the wine in a restaurant to give the go-ahead to the waiter. I have never had the temerity to demur.

Although I escaped his ministrations in the nets, 'Old Phiggy', as we disrespectfully dubbed him behind his back, had a lasting influence on my attitude to cricket. One warm afternoon, the strong sunshine emphasizing the dust on the Reform Bill and the Repeal of the Corn Laws, he closed our history books and read to us instead the immortal chapter of the cricket match in A.G. Macdonell's *England Their England*. For my money, this inspired piece of slapstick will always rank as one of the most felicitously brilliant passages of comic writing, albeit by a Scot, in the English language. The revelation left me gasping and tearful. What I had hitherto regarded as a dull imposition, calling for unattainable talent and impossible dedication, was glimpsed as a source of fun, even joy. St Paul, as he approached Damascus, would have understood my shock.

Years later, during my undergraduate days at Cambridge, my father, as president of the local cricket club, was required to field a side against his own fairly competent Village XI. I was instructed to recruit a team. As most of my sporting friends were rowing men, a pastime at which I had at last found some natural ability and small success, the resulting squad was more accomplished at wielding pint pots than bat and ball, but in the event there was ample scope for both.

Dad had a notoriously difficult ear to bite when I needed to borrow a fiver, but he was lavishly hospitable when it came to entertaining my friends. The Village Match became an annual institution, prized more for the memorable shindigs than the stroke-play. The Visitors would assemble in the 'Robin Hood' on the Friday evening, to the gratification of the amiable landlord. Albert had been severely wounded in the war and was reputed to be 'leather from the ribs down', but he dispensed a demonstrably potable brew with long suffering geniality.

Supper, when the gathering was finally hauled across the road to the Cottage, was traditionally a Yorkshire dish, a recipe of my grandmother's known as 'Blanks and Prizes'. I pass it on gratuitously. It consists quite simply of broad beans (our vegetable garden was still bountiful) and lumps of ham, a ratio of about ten to one, in a parsley sauce. The beans were the blanks and the ham supplied the prizes. In palmier days it was a poor man's dish.

I think it was A.P. Herbert who claimed that golf is a marvellous game to be bad at, because you get so many chances to hit the ball. The reverse is true of cricket, especially if you are a tail-ender on a winning side. We never won. This did mean that as a permanent last-wicket batsman I had my brief moments of glory. Not that the side was composed entirely of duffers. A Cambridge fast bowler and accomplished portrait artist, later capped for Lancashire, was persuaded to slum it by the promise of ale, and some of the oarsmen showed a surprising aptitude for the willow. By and large, however, they were a motley bunch, mostly wanting to field in the deep so they could smoke.

There is one advantage which offsets the ignominy of batting last. It is a lonely, menaced journey on the way out to the wicket, but you have lots of jolly company on the way back. For my most memorable innings I left my companions, remarking like the gallant Captain Oates that I was going for a little walk, and adding unconvincingly that I could be away some time. My fellow batsman was Henry Clark, then MP for North Antrim before he was ousted by a certain energetic clergyman. 'Just stay in, James,' he said, 'and let me do the work.' Two balls to face and he made it sound easy. The first delivery was a fast cannonball. Hopefully I stuck my bat in the way and it glanced off the edge past fine leg for four runs. Hope soared and I blocked the last ball of the over as the clock struck six. Henry checked with his watch, and with a shout of 'Good God, Jim, they're open!' – promptly ran me out. It was the highest score I have ever made.

The late Fifties found me back at Malsis in a teaching capacity. Once more I was spending summer afternoons cricketing, now umpiring on the Donkey Field. Again, discreetly screened by trees from the experts on the top field, I nursed a bunch of haymakers. Remembering my own days of drudgery I was resolved to impart the fun. These stalwarts were the Gentlemen of the Third Game. Our totem was an enormous cricket bat some nine inches wide, surmounted by our motto, ' 'Tis better to have loafed and lost than never to have loafed at all'. Though talent (for cricket) was limited, we had exaggerated respect for protocol and the gentlemanly behaviour which should be inseparable from the game. As mounting scores consisted mainly of extras – wides and byes in equal proportion – and a 'long-stop' was considered infra-dig, the boys invented a distinctive fielding position deep behind the wicket-keeper known simply as 'plug'. This proliferated into extra plug, cover plug and even silly plug.

The position looked even sillier on one occasion when an energetic bowler, bowling towards the short boundary end, misjudged his length and sent the ball rocketing in a lofty arc over the bushes into the middle of the drive. This was undoubtedly a 'six-bye', but as I needed three arms to signal it to the scorer, the feat remains unrecorded in the annals of cricket. Many and unchronicled were the exploits of that gallant band. Maybe as we approach what must be a silver jubilee some former Gentleman will take up his pen and write a definitive history. I suggest 'Not Cricket, Chaps!' as a suitably modest title.

In the meantime I must return to my own history. 1945 was

dominated by great events on the world stage and each day seemed
to bring new excitement – a match on unparalleled scale and one
which events seemed to suggest that we would win. Another letter
home from Tim, unlike his elder brother a promising cricketer, only
just predates the European victory and only just gives it priority.

Friday May 4th, 1945.

Dear Mum and Daddy,

Thankyou for the postcard that you sent me. The
blue tits were very nice. Hitler is dead and Mussolini was
murdered and Gobbles committed suiside we heard. On the
news it said that Berlin is fallen. We have not had a game of
cricket this term yet, so I hope we will have one this
afternoon. We go in the canals now, but we cannot play with
the railways for we haven't got the trains. In break we play
catching a cricket ball with one of the big boys. Mr Phillips is
just now getting the big game ready. I hope he will get ours
ready too! Tell Daddy I hope he gets some good meals in
London, and some time off to enjoy himself too.

Cheerio! and all my love,

Tim

(P.S.) If you ever see Sambo the cat give her my love.

The canals referred to a life-like working model of a canal built
along one side of a long glazed conservatory which stretched the fifty
yards between the house and the gym. The other side housed a
Hornby railway. The tiled floor made a splendid roller-skating rink. It
was here that I was permitted to keep my breeding cages, rear my
caterpillars and hatch my moths. Many of the chrysalids had travelled north with me, but the grounds were well planted with trees
and an ornamental lake was overgrown with bushes and wild
flowers which, in the absence of pesticides and weedkillers, supported a fair variety of caterpillar life. The mouldings and crevices in
the stonework of the school building provided hiding places for well
camouflaged cocoons, and at last the blackout was over and moths
were attracted to the dormitories by the light.

I used to venture further afield when, about every three weeks, we
had a 'Going-out Sunday'. The three of us would spend these days of

liberty with our grandparents, and get out on the moors to see what we could collect. Home cooking, escape from the discipline and routine of school, and recovery of a sense of belonging to a family rather than a regiment made these brief furloughs infinitely precious.

One boy at this time came back from a Sunday out clutching an authentic olive and brown silk parachute. This furnished exhilarating sport for a while, billowing across the top field on breezy days with a score of boys clinging to the cords, dragged along in an attempt to anchor it. Alas, the owner, inflated by his new popularity, became unbearably capricious in deciding which fickle friend of the moment could or could not join him in the game. Fed up ultimately with such wayward behaviour, one gusty day at a given signal we all let go, leaving the hapless parachutist solo, to soar alarmingly into the air. Luckily the tall sycamores bordering the cricket square frustrated his imminent flight into Lancashire. The parachute was confiscated after this and the owner ordered to take it home, but he remains one of the few ever to have climbed down a tree without the preliminary effort of climbing up it.

Going-out Sundays acquired wider scope for adventure when, in May 1946, my grandparents moved from the Skipton house into Wharfedale, to a little white stone cottage in Threshfield. Junior by about a century to our Hertfordshire home, originally a keeper's cottage in the extensive seventeenth-century deer park, Rose Cottage peered over the wall through its roses and clematis at the ancient stocks on a small green triangle known grandly as Threshfield Park. Though now a busy route for lime lorries and tourists, the village was then a sleepy collection of sheep and dairy farms. Milk was not delivered; instead you went to the dairy to collect your jug, left there the night before, protected by a little veil of bead-edged muslin to keep the flies off.

The river was handy, and under Gramp's tutelage my skill with the fishing rod developed steadily. I had graduated from casting practice on the lawn at Raikes Lea, trying to land a single point-fly on a dinner-plate. One triumphant day I had lowered the fly gently on to the plate three times in succession and jumped up and down in glee. Gramp had watched the hat-trick from the house and strode out through the French windows. Without comment he stuck a penny stamp in the centre of the plate, stood back a yard or two and cast the fly unerringly on to the stamp. However I was considered proficient enough to move on to the river without embarrassing anybody.

Not only was my grandfather President of the Linton, Threshfield and Grassington Angling Club, he was also captain of the local domino team which trained across the road in the Old Hall Inn. The Old Hall was then kept by one Alex Higgins, known throughout the Dales as 'The Duke', a sturdy ex-bruiser with a voice like a shorthorn bull. On first acquaintance his attempts at geniality towards us three frankly terrified me. I gradually came to realize, however, that his Yorkshire bark was far worse than his bite. On a visit once to London, Alex called in at No. 97, Harley Street, hoping to lure my father out for a lunchtime pint. Dad was not in, and the receptionist asked if she could take a message. 'Aye – tell him t'Duke o' Threshfield called to see him!' was the rejoinder. The good lady dearly loved a lord – not a few celebrities visited No. 97 – and enquired of Dad on his return the blood and lineage of the Duke of Threshfield. 'Ah!' said my father airily, 'we have adjoining estates in Yorkshire.'

Early in 1947 I achieved the distinction of promotion to the 1st XV, but it was a curtailed season. The new year ushered in one of the severest winters on record. The arctic weather combined with post-war austerity to bring the country almost to a stop. It is often difficult to place events in their respective years, but everyone over fifty remembers the winter of '47. Coal was in short supply and the railways, not to say the roads, were frequently at a standstill. Our bread and supplies were hauled up the drive on huge bracken sledges from one of the neighbouring farms. Days were spent tobogganing on the hills and skating on the lake. To refer again to Tim's chronicles, 'As the afternoon arrives the shrill voices of muscular youth ring out and on to the frozen pond pour excited boys eager for the fun. Lithe figures skim across the ice and experienced skaters glide gracefully.' He had a tendency towards the purple at the time.

Even winter sports began to pall. Snow-drifts seventeen to twenty feet deep lined the lanes, leaving farms and cottages regularly buried as high as the upstairs windows. Every night brought more snow, and all had to be dug out anew the next day. Many lessons were abandoned for digging parties. I remember a day when even the sledge stuck, and we positioned ourselves down the steep part of the drive, holding on to a long rope like alpine mountaineers, and passed the day's loaves from hand to hand up to the front door. Another day when the gods were in particularly sarcastic vein we trekked out with shovels to rescue the local snow plough and rode triumphantly back on it.

Hundreds of sheep, with lambing imminent, were lost. The snow on the moors, high above the hidden wall tops, became impacted and we could walk up the glacial sweeps unimpeded. Directly above a buried stone wall the snow, retaining doubtless some conducted heat, was soft and the unwary walker would suddenly disappear up to the armpits. In March, after two months of ice-age, we toured the Dales with Dad on a free Sunday. The countryside was a polar landscape. Traffic into Wharfedale vanished through a snow tunnel in the little village of Rylstone. Eventually we reached Hardraw in Wensleydale and clambered through drifts to the high force, one of the tallest unbroken falls in Europe. Astoundingly it was a single huge icicle, a towering, fluted column of glass cascading without motion one hundred feet from the layered scar top above into the pyramidal snow-drift concealing the dark pool below.

In contrast the summer of 1947 was marked by long spells of hot, dry, sunny weather. I think everyone was in need of some kind of gala. Although, thankfully, the dangerous threat to life had subsided, peacetime, after the first joyful celebrations, was proving to be as sombre as the war, but without the enlivening excitement. The therapeutic spree was provided, as often happens, by the Monarchy. Princess Elizabeth's wedding to Prince Philip, notably celebrated by us with a whole-holiday, was the cue for forgetting gloom and looking forward cheerfully to the future.

As time went by, life returned to normal English things. Bananas came back on the scene the following year, and the great Bradman brought his touring side from Australia. New idols emerged. The crowing conceit of the Lancastrian faction, when a youngster named Hilton twice bowled out the Don for a duck in the Australia v. Lancs match, knew no bounds. The pervasive influence of the Test matches was displayed at its keenest when one devotee identified, in a Scripture exam, the three participants of the burning, fiery furnace as Shadrach, Meshach and Toshack.

1948 found me working hard for a scholarship to Sedbergh. At the same time post-war depression was finally dispelled when London hosted the 1948 Olympic Games, the first since the brazen propaganda feast in Hitler's Berlin. Life and attitudes have changed in the forty years since, and the Games typify the revolution. This was the last great amateur contest. No commercialism, politics, flag-wagging or drugs left the aftertaste one has come to expect, and RAF Nissen huts served as the now obligatory prestigious Olympic Village. The British squad actually had a training weekend at Butlins at Clacton. Oarsmen Wilson and Laurie briefly returned from their lives in the

Sudan to win the Silver Goblets at Henley and then the Olympic Double Sculls. Emil Zatopek, popular hero, trained for the marathon in army boots. Fanny Blankers-Koen won four golds for Holland and travelled to Wembley on the Tube, almost missing her final contest after an over-long shopping trip in the West End. Germany was, of course, not represented, but we felt it just that (still unrepatriated) prisoners-of-war had been put to work on the preparations. Professionalism may have improved results and records beyond measure, but an innocence has been lost.

Another loss is the rustic railway on which I travelled to compete in the scholarship examination. Kildwick Station was just down the road, and the train, calling at a string of stations now extinct, wandered north out of Airedale into Ribblesdale, briefly into Lancashire and Westmorland, then back into Yorkshire again to deposit me at Sedbergh – or, to be accurate, about a mile short of it. The trains must have been more *ventre-à-terre* when the stations were built, for, once north of Settle, wooden steps had to be brought to the carriage doors to help passengers negotiate the three-foot drop to the platforms. The fells were higher than my familiar moors. It was hot and sultry, and swifts chased each other, squealing, between the houses. At rest on a wall in the evening sunshine – a propitious omen I thought – was a Herald moth, its deeply scalloped wings frosted with orange on a purple ground. I have it yet.

A few weeks later I heard with happy relief that I had won my scholarship, a fitting end to months of study. I finally left Malsis, and spent a relaxed summer holiday in Hertfordshire, in Sussex and on the Isle of Wight among my butterflies and moths, with scarcely a thought of the new pages so soon to open.

4

Of Grubs
and Greepy Grawlies

Puss moth caterpillar

On a moonless July night in the hot dry summer of 1947, an eerie white light shimmered in the overgrown north-west corner of the churchyard in our Hertfordshire village, where the River Beane drifted sluggishly past an untidy little grove of immature poplars. The glow illuminated a sheet hung from one of the trees and silhouetted three figures as they moved in stealthy shadow play in front of it. Ghost hunters? Jerry Cruncher and his nefarious gang? The furtive quiet was shattered as, with an eldritch shriek, a white staring face, suddenly spotlit, materialized above one of the taller headstones behind the fence. The three figures fled in panic.

Only on one susbsequent occasion have I been so irrationally frightened, and again I was skirting a churchyard. I had been fishing on the River Wharfe below Linton Church. The sun had set and my dusky path home lay over a stile and past the old tombstones. I heard a very human cough and in the gloom beyond from one of those low walled plots which, with a stone at head and feet, look like a gravel filled bed, a figure heaved itself up. You hear of people 'rooted to the spot', and the cliché is startling in its accuracy. For a moment reason fled and the explicable world of cause and effect vanished in a wild, noiseless explosion. Then a deep-throated and indignant 'Baa-a-a!' restored sanity as a large ewe bolted off into the darkness and I laughed, with relief and not a little hysteria, loud and long among the uncaring sleepers.

On the earlier adventure we had left the cottage in the small hours through a bedroom window and climbed down over the porch, leaving suitable humped forms under our bedclothes to allay suspicion. Armed with a lantern, we were out to do a bit of night mothing. The visitor who so alarmed us was our old acquaintance the barn owl, out for a spot of hunting on his own account and demanding to know who had dared 'molest his ancient, solitary reign'. It was time to pack up anyway, and we collected our paraphernalia and, still shaken, stole back home again.

The foolish moth burning her wings in the candle flame has been held up as a salutory warning from time immemorial, but just why moths should be attracted to light is far from clear. Not all species come to the light, and some nights are 'mothier' than others. When you consider that moths are far older in the evolutionary timetable than we are, artificial light is for them a very recent development. The answer must lie in the natural world; such behaviour is an accidental response to a phenomenon not catered for in their millions of years of selection and adaptation.

When I was a schoolboy at Sedbergh I met the great geneticist, the late Dr E.B. Ford, who probably knew more about butterflies and moths than anybody else around at the time. He was giving a talk on heredity and illustrated it with a bright collection of Jersey Tiger moths, large gaudy beauties with forewings streaked with chocolate and white and hindwings scarlet with black spots, which excited my envy. Afterwards I put the puzzle to him. He held the opinion that moths fly to the moon. This smacked of one of the more complicated adventures of Dr Dolittle, but he explained that he was testing the theory, with the help of the RAF, on an island, using a captive balloon which was illuminated from below by a searchlight. Certainly moths were attracted to it on nights when the moon was dark, some species to considerable heights in an attempt to reach their goal.

It is a case of the old, old story, and sex would seem to lie at the base of the behaviour, though Dr Ford termed it 'dispersal of genetic material'. Simply, moths fly high on moonlit nights, where they meet a wider choice of partners than among the restricting terrain at ground level. In Yorkshire, night-flying moths were known without distinction as 'bustards', and two or three big woolly artificial flies which imitate them have inherited the name. Bustard fishing is an exciting sport, a chuck-and-chance-it technique carried out from a secure spot on the river bank in pitch darkness. Significantly it is quite useless to go bustard fishing when there is a moon, and the same goes for night mothing.

Hunting for caterpillars at night with a torch might seem to be carrying enthusiasm rather too far, but the game has many advantages. Apart from sheer bluff, and I shall come to that later, most caterpillars have no obviously defensive weapons and come out of hiding to feed at night, in comparative security from the army of predators and parasitic wasps which constantly threaten them. Many animals are at their most active at night, and the goings-on even in your own garden, when you are snugly tucked up, could well surprise you.

My wife and I, in common with millions of other gardeners, wage a constant – often losing – battle against slugs. Slug bait is limited in its effect, leaves a glutinous mess where it strikes and has me worried about the pets and the visiting birds who might inadvertently swallow it. Rings of soot, fortifications of sharp gravel, inverted grapefruit skins, saucers of beer (the only predilection in which the slug and I are in unqualified agreement) – all just scratch the surface of the problem. The only really satisfactory method is a wicked pair of scissors and a torch.

I am a humane man. Conservation is high in my list of priorities, and I tread carefully like the Brahmin who fears lest he crush the least of God's creatures beneath his feet. I will gently rescue beetles from the bath tub, transport woodlice by the wheelbarrow load to safer and more convenient playgrounds, but slicing slugs is a form of genocide I indulge in without the slightest compunction. Like any other criminal, the slug prefers the hours of darkness for his fell purposes. On warm summer nights, when the thoughts of saner people are more romantically inclined, Wendy and I tiptoe round the dahlias, snipping viciously.

Another advantage of darkness for spotting caterpillars is directly associated with their defensive camouflage. The sun highlights an animal from above, leaving its belly in shadow, so in daylight a dark back merging into a pale tummy will counteract the shading and confuse the shape to the onlooker. Shining a torch from below reverses the cryptic shading, and a leaf-green larva, safely concealed in the daylight, will stand out in strong relief at night.

In July and August we would search the poplars near the church, in permitted, daylight hours, for the caterpillars of the Puss moth. The moth itself is quite large, a pale whitish colour and covered in copious white-grey fluff like a Persian cat. It has three smaller but similar cousins known as Kittens. We found both the Poplar Kitten and the Sallow Kitten in our quest for the Puss caterpillar. Few contrasts in the moth world are as vivid as that between the fluffy, friendly Puss and its grotesque-looking larva. I have on more than one occasion had one brought to me for identification by people who didn't even recognize it as a caterpillar. Pale emerald green, it has a dark brown-purple saddle, white-edged, on its rear end and a pointed hood just behind the head, tipped with the same purple. A bright red collar sports two black false eyes. The other end divides into a pair of retractable thin red tails. When alarmed, the caterpillar lifts both ends clear of its perch and, like a tortoise, pulls its head into the hood. While this gives the demonic impression of a gaping, red maw, at the same time it whips the tails forward over its back; a truly frightening apparition and a superb piece of bluff.

It shows the same unorthodox ingenuity when chrysalling up (a phrase which we borrowed from the Keeper at Wicken Fen). It chews up the bark of the poplar bole and makes a bark cocoon, a rigid undetectable bump. Nor does the cunning stop here. The small panel through which the adult will emerge is purposely made paper thin. The chrysalis is fitted with a knife-edged device which will cut its way clear, and the moth exudes a softening fluid which finally effects its escape. The moth was not uncommon, and with such elaborate precautions at every stage, who can wonder? We would provide pieces of bark as caterpillars reached maturity, for they were quite capable of munching their way into the wood of the breeding cage when their time came to pupate.

The Puss and the Kittens belong to a family termed the *Notodontidae*, or the Prominents. Most of their caterpillars are to some degree unusual, jaggedly humped and scaled like the backs of heraldic dragons, and contrive to look as unconventional as possible, as do the moths. I once, at Malsis, reared a Pale Prominent and one day found the empty pupal case but no moth. Sabotage? At last I found it, where it had been all the time, when what appeared to be a chip of pale dead wood began to move its drying wings.

We found the strangest Prominent of all in Eastbourne on a crab-apple tree in the garden. This was the caterpillar of the Lobster moth. A dull brown in colour, with the familiar dorsal row of tiger tooth humps, the rear end is swollen into a convincing lobster claw, arching forwards over the back. To complete the deception the real legs are thick and elongated and waggle menacingly when the caterpillar is disturbed. In this case the bluff is reinforced with a more practical defence. The caterpillar can actually squirt formic acid in times of stress – the breeding cage smelt quite strongly of it – and this chemical warfare combined with its crustacean disguise must deter many a bird hoping for a quick snack. Sadly the Lobster caterpillar took sick and died, and we never found another.

The Prominents have bodies shaped to achieve their cryptic fronts, but many other caterpillars rely on hair to do the same job. We have already met two of the Tussocks, or the family *Lymantriidae*, the Vapourer and the Gold Tail, and there is one other member of this family which I considered the most lavishly beautiful of all the caterpillars I had seen. The species in this case was the larva of the Pale Tussock, known to generations of migrant cockney field labourers as the Hop Dog. The Pale Tussock was often common enough in the hopfields of Kent to be considered a minor menace. We found them on the wild hops, which grew fairly plentifully in the hedges both in Hertfordshire and Sussex, the flowers like soft green fir-cones with a fragrant beery scent when crushed.

The caterpillar, about an inch and a half in length, is a pale lime green, fringed with long whitish hairs. Four shaving-brush tussocks of lemon yellow stand erect from the middle of the back and a red plumed tuft from the tail. Offsetting this pretty array, the spaces between the segments, peeping out when the caterpillar is extended, are black. It was the contention of the early Impressionists that the colour black does not occur in nature. I go along with that, and I never include black on my palette. Black velvet gets pretty near, but even here there is a suspicion of reflected light. However, the rings of the Hop Dog give the lie to the theory. When I first encountered the caterpillar, I thought with surprise that here was the deepest impenetrable black I had ever seen. In fact I thought that the caterpillar, resting quietly on a leaf, had been cut clean through in two places.

A moth which can wreak havoc on your currant and gooseberry bushes is the Magpie moth. It flies by day, and with its broad wings, white with chains of black blobs relieved by deep yellow, and slender waist it might easily be mistaken for a butterfly. We thought these moths were a bit wet, for whenever we disturbed one, poking with a stick in the hedgerow (it also lays its eggs on sloe and hawthorn), it would fall down and pretend to be dead. It is possible that birds prefer a live meal to a dead one, and that playing possum is safer than trying to escape. Black and yellow, though, are traditional warning colours and advise predators that the moths have an unpleasant taste. The caterpillars, also marked strikingly on their white bodies with black and red, make no attempt to hide but rather advertise their unpalatable presence.

It would clearly be unprofitable to be protected by a repellent taste without proclaiming the fact. After all, a savage peck will put an end to you whether you are spat out afterwards or not. Black and yellow are highly popular as distinctive warning colours. A young swallow may be stung once by a wasp, and will thereafter avoid the tiger stripes. The caterpillars of the Cinnabar moth are also striped garishly in yellow and black. Often found in huge numbers, they can defoliate their foodplant. As this is the common ragwort, which itself contains a poisonous alkaloid, noxious to cattle, nobody is likely to dispute their sole right to it.

'Safety in numbers' is an old maxim, and the Cinnabars swear by it. An inexperienced bird may take one of these gaudy snacks, but the others will be left severely alone. The loss of one individual that the many may survive is a law which nature, careless of individuals but jealous for the genes as a whole, implements universally. I remember one gruesome expedition in the early 1950s when we

crossed the Downs on our bicycles between Jevington and Alfriston.
The man-induced epidemic of myxomatosis was at its height. The
ragwort was rife and every plant was host to its cluster of munching
Cinnabar caterpillars in enormous numbers. Also munching, still
incredibly cropping the short turf with a ghastly intensity although
they were blind and purulent, swollen and half paralysed, were
hundreds of miserable rabbits. We had come across one or two
solitary sufferers before, and with a swift cuff put each out of its pain,
but this scene of horror was more than we could begin to cope with.
We couldn't even avoid cycling over them.

Other gregarious caterpillars there are who, for their early infant
life anyway, elect to co-exist in large numbers. As they have no in-
built protection, they spin communal tents on the foodplant and
take their nourishment inside a webby crèche. Among these are the
larvae of the Lackey moth. An aspect of the moths which tickles my
curiosity is how many of their familar names reflect our forgotten
past. The Alchymist and the Short Cloaked moth, the Quaker and
the Nonconformist, the Cousin German, Lutestring, Shuttle Shaped
Dart and the True Lovers' Knot all evoke bygone images. The Lackey,
a pale ginger, furrily stocky little moth, is so called, I conceive, on
account of the handsome caterpillars. These wear lengthwise stripes
of powder blue, white, red and orange, like the colourful livery of the
servants of some opulent nobleman. They live in a tent, but on fine
days love to sit on the outside of it to sunbathe and show off their gala
dress.

The Footmen are a family of moths which also echo domestic
servants of the past. They have narrow wings, which at rest they fold
closely round the body in a stiff tube, as though standing rigidly to
attention. They have had the wit to dodge competition by laying
their eggs on lichens, giving their caterpillars a diet unsought by
rival species. The Footmen are closely related to the showy Tiger
moths, and here again I suspect the name refers to the bright waistcoats and striped livery of the grooms and pages, nicknamed tigers, of
long ago, for the moths are not striated in black and yellow like the
big cats.

The lengthways stripes of the Lackey seem to be purely decorative,
but others use them to good purpose. The Broom moth caterpillar,
common enough but which we found in profusion in the gardens of
Woolwich War Memorial Hospital, is brown or sometimes dark
green, with narrow stripes of yellow, red and black. We enjoyed
visits to Woolwich, waiting for Dad to finish his operating list, as the

gardens were quite rewarding. I remember standing on the imposing front steps one evening in the dusk, trying (and failing) to catch the hunting bats in our butterfly nets. The caterpillars needed a close search, for their stripes merged perfectly, aligned with the ridged broom stalks.

A further Woolwich prize was the caterpillar of the Sycamore moth. For some reason very few moths choose sycamore as a foodplant and the caterpillars enjoy a relatively exclusive claim. The rather nondescript grey moth blends well with the sycamore bark, but the larva is one of the glamour pusses of the caterpillar world. It has a long silky mane of red-gold hair, gathered in pointed locks either side of a chain of white, black-edged triangles down the middle of the back. When it curls up, as it does readily when disturbed, it looks like a dangerous, spiky gold button. We found the first sycamore caterpillar beneath the tree, a grubby, bedraggled chap which we couldn't identify. Overnight in the breeding cage it changed its skin, discarding the shabby old coat, and revealed its glory in a brand-new blonde fur.

The hairiest of all, and a close relation, is the caterpillar of the Miller. Another link with a vanished past, it is a dusty, floury white. The moth is a dusty dove-grey but, like the Sycamore, it is not particularly distinctive. I found my caterpillar on low scrub birch in a Sussex wood and I had to look closely two or three times before I decided it was indeed a caterpillar. The hairs are as long as the body, cascading downwards from the sides and brushed forwards from its back to curve gracefully round the head on the starboard side and backwards symmetrically round the tail on the port. The effect is of a curled, downy feather, no meal for a hungry bird.

What we called the 'Big League' of hairies is the family *Lasio-campidae*, of which the Lackey moths are junior members. Some of the moths are of considerable size, and their caterpillars are correspondingly large. Apart from the ichneumon flies, the ghoulish parasitic wasps, these giants have few natural predators when full grown, and therefore little need to hide. Their chief enemy is the cuckoo. This unorthodox harbinger of summer has a throat adapted to a diet of hairy caterpillars. It is this, rather than laziness, which has persuaded it to foster out its young, for baby cuckoos need more readily digested fare, the sort of insects provided for their own young by robins and reed warblers and meadow pipits.

The Fox moth, which crops up at regular intervals throughout my narrative, is a member of this family, and another is the Drinker moth. The unusual habit of the Drinker, whose caterpillar takes refreshment from dewdrops on the coarse grasses on which it feeds, was noticed in the seventeenth century, and the English name is an old one. Linnaeus called it *'potatoria'*, the tippler. The moths are very active, especially the males, and rearing them from caterpillars was the safest way of getting perfect specimens.

The caterpillars of the Oak Eggar were not uncommon in our haunts both in Hertfordshire and later in Sussex. They do feed on oak, as the name suggests, for we once reared a cageful on oak leaves, but we found them mostly on hawthorn hedges, where they seemed quite happy to eat the interweaving blackberry leaves as well. They are very handsome – a silvery grey underneath ginger fur and jet black in the ring divisions – and fall off when disturbed, curled up tight like an ammonite. The females are all at least half as big again as the males, a characteristic of this moth family as a whole, and this helps to sex the caterpillar. If it reaches over three inches it is going to be a female. On the Yorkshire moors we found a sturdy cousin, the Northern Eggar, almost identical but even bigger.

The cocoon which the Oak Eggar spins to protect itself in the chrysalis state is large and hard like a dark oval pebble. A chrysalis is not entirely dormant and lifeless. It can wriggle its abdominal segments from side to side quite effectively. In our early days we would pick up each chrysalis fairly regularly and squeeze it till it moved, 'to see if it was still alive'. This probably resulted in the demise of not a few. If you can bear it, the safest test is gently to touch it with the tip of your tongue. A live chrysalis will feel distinctly cold. When the first Oak Eggar we reared, a female, spun her tough sarcophagus, she attached it by a flimsy web under a ledge in the breeding cage, from where it had to be extricated to make way for the next occupiers. The chrysalis inside vibrated violently as we held the cocoon, giving our hands what seemed a sudden, startling electric shock.

The biggest of the Big League is the caterpillar of the Lappet moth. There is something intimidating about its enormous size when full grown, but like all the others it is quite harmless. The first we ever saw was on a bank near Sinjun's Wood, but alas it was covered by the small cocoons of ichneumon fly grubs which had erupted through its skin. The sorry monster was still alive and moving, but its hours were numbered. The mature caterpillar – again the female is much larger than the male – can reach nearly five inches in length, thick and heavy, a dark grey covered in black flecks. Tufts of dark hair sprout from fleshy protuberances low down along its length, the 'lappets' which give it its name. I once found, my diary tells me, a batch of twenty-two eggs on honeysuckle in Abbot's Wood near Eastbourne, in the June of 1951. The usual foodplant was blackthorn, and in captivity we fed them on apple from the garden, often in a muslin 'sleeve' on the tree.

The eggs are quite distinctive, about the size of small lead shot, white and prettily marbled with concentric rings of dark purple. I added my own illustrations to the reference book, for I discovered something that none of the books told me. The caterpillars when first hatched were about a quarter of an inch long. They have some hefty growing to do. As caterpillars develop they grow out of their skins and go through a series of 'moults', in which the old skin splits and is shed, often resulting in a complete change of appearance. The baby Lappets, until the first moult, were a velvet black with long whitish hairs, and the intersegmental rings were lemon yellow. I would not have been able to identify them in the open.

Our young Lappet caterpillars were not infrequently found as a result of a form of caterpillar hunting known alarmingly as 'beating'. The method is not as brutal as it sounds, the necessary apparatus consisting of a walking stick and an old umbrella. The open and inverted umbrella is pushed in under, say, a blackthorn bush, and the stick is used to give the bush a few sudden, brisk taps. Caterpillars taken unawares lose their grasp and tumble down into the umbrella, which saves a lot of staring and leaf examination. Most of the haul would be small fry – larger ones are not so easily dislodged – but the luck of the game could be exciting. Two things are important. One must note what particular food plant any batch comes from, and afterwards the umbrella should be held over the bush and tapped, to empty back any unwanted larvae.

By far the most likely caterpillars to fall into our beating trap were 'loopers' of many different species. These, the *Geometridae*, are the 'inchworms' of America which Danny Kaye sang about, 'measuring the marigolds'. They have dispensed with their false 'prolegs' in the middle of the body, retaining only the claspers at the tail end. The Magpie moths on your gooseberry bushes are typical loopers. To move along, they loop the body, bringing the claspers up just behind the real legs. They hold on with the claspers and reach forward with the front end, as one might measure a length of cloth, spanning with thumb and little finger. Some move like this with remarkable speed.

The family is truly a huge one, and many of them are expert mimics. With no protruding prolegs, what simpler way to avoid detection than to hang on tight with the claspers, stretch out straight and imitate a twig! Among the hundreds that adopt such a disguise, probably the most successful is the Oak Beauty, a lovely moth, barred and speckled with pepper and salt, which flies very early in the year. The caterpillar is so exactly a replica of an oak twig, with bumps and patches of colour just where the leaf buds occur, that it promotes the strong suspicion that what we think of as chance evolution must have a supreme intelligence lurking somewhere behind it.

The Large Emerald moth has a similarly bumped, twiggy caterpillar. It hibernates in winter Before this the caterpillar is brown and matches the autumn foliage of birch or hazel. When it continues life in the spring, its next moult changes it to a leafy green colour for the rest of its larval life. Its little cousin, the exquisite Small Emerald, feeds on the wild clematis, known (why?) as traveller's joy and, when the seeds mature, as the old man's beard. Throughout its life it mimics a stiff, green shoot. The Geometers embrace more than four hundred species in our country alone, each with its patterns precisely ordained.

Although nowadays I release my hatched insects, I still cannot resist rearing caterpillars. They have so many more, man-induced perils to contend with than when I was a boy, that I feel justified in this. I 'rescued' a sizeable colony of caterpillars of the Small Tortoiseshell butterfly only last summer, before the nettles on which I found them were sprayed and destroyed, and they not only emerged without a single casualty but rewarded me by staying in the garden to grace the buddleia and the ice plants. Many later found their way into the house to hibernate.

Once safely hatched, a pair will often quickly mate in captivity and provide fertile eggs for another year's nurselings, but no cage is capacious enough in a normal household to contain a moth or butterfly. If the release involves an excursion to the right habitat, so be it, but responsibility must extend to the final farewell. Caterpillars are rewarding if unresponsive charges. They don't need taking for walks and, if a good supply of fresh food is provided, you can happily leave them for the week-end. Little did we guess, infants reading the strange tale of the 'Grawlies' in its old Victorian binding, that the creatures would come to haunt us in reality. They proved a fascinating and integral part of our boyhood and an insight to one of the most intriguing life cycles in the natural world. As so often, Tim summed it up in a drawing. Two caterpillars on a leaf were staring mistrustfully at a moth planing close overhead. One was saying 'You'll never get *me* up in one of those things!'

5

A Stern Nurse

Moorland moths
(left to right) Beautiful Yellow Underwing; Fox moth;
Common Heath; Pebble Hook Tip; Ruby Tiger

On A SULTRY DAY IN SEPTEMBER 1948, ONE OF THOSE OPPRESSIVE London days when heat radiated from the pavements and I would envy Kipling's rhinoceros who could actually unbutton and remove his skin, I arrived with the family at Euston to be deposited on the Carlisle train. London made no concessions to warm weather in those days. To walk abroad in the West End without a jacket would have laid one open to calumny; a 'T' shirt would probably have led to arrest. Shirts with collars attached were considered very casual. I and my fellows were initiated into the mysteries of collar-studs and cuff links, both of which we found constricting and irksome on this day of new experiences.

Until he achieved some kind of status and badge of rank, the Sedbergh tyro wore a plain black tie. The lady at the news stall where I bought myself a new Saint book for the journey looked sympathetic and hoped it would cheer me up. I realized that the sight of my funeral tie and foreboding countenance had convinced her I had suffered some bereavement. This, I reflected, as the train moved out and I waved goodbye to my parents and to Tim and Patrick receding with the platform, was all too true. Albeit surrounded by a score or two of similarly clad strangers in the reserved compartment, for the first time in my life I was on my own.

Rugby, Crewe, Warrington, Wigan, Preston – I didn't guess on that first journey how this litany was to imprint itself on my memory over the next five years. Air travel to distant climes often brings a traumatic change as passengers dressed for Manchester disembark into the balmy air of Madeira or Marrakesh, but on a more insular scale I still recall the involuntary jolt as one opened the carriage door to the cooler airs and harsher accents of the North. On this occasion we left the train at Carnforth and bundled into the Sedbergh bus. This was my first encounter with Sid Braithwaite, a character who could have stepped, like Jimmy James or Frank Randall, straight off the music-hall stage and who, with his haphazardly opportunist style of driving, put the fear of God into more Sedberghians than ever did their more tyrannical masters and pastors.

The bus, a time-worn charabanc, had a canvas top stretched over hoops, the kind of vehicle seen in fading photographs in countless Yorkshire pubs surrounded by intently staring, heavy moustached ghosts and bearing such captions as 'Bay Horse trip, 1911'. Our luggage was stowed aboard by the simple but effective procedure of slinging it outside on the roof. Once inside, the bulges in the canvas overhead attested to the continued presence of the bags and marked their progress. At one stage of the cross-country route there is a steep hill known as Scots Jeans. Here we careered, gears protesting and exhaust firing salvoes, down the impossible gradient. Alarmingly the bulges towards the stern had smoothed out and the forward canopy was fast acquiring new ones. Sid negotiated the descent with his face screwed back towards his anxious passengers, gleefully propounding his philosophy of life, 'It'll be reight!' Sid's brother, Gentleman George, whom I was to meet later, was the other half of this memorable double act; immaculately dark-suited, his hair slicked down like a bandleader's, he ran what was to become a thriving bus company in the years to come.

The first sinking impression of School House as I walked through the bare tarmac yard was of blind windows faced with bars and iron grilles. That these were a protection to keep footballs and cricket balls out rather than the inmates in was not immediately apparent. The new boys had arrived a day before the beginning of term, so the house was almost deserted and three cell-like doors opposite a spartan bath house directly inside the heavy, studded entrance door accentuated the atmosphere of the penitentiary. Intriguingly I found each narrow cell contained a piano. 'Dura Virum Nutrix', proclaimed the school motto. A voice in my ear supplied an impromptu translation: 'To endure it a man must be nuts!' A sturdy little Scot joined me in convulsed laughter at his inspired piece of dog Latin, until we were coldly informed by a supercilious Head of House, who had overheard him, that the correct version was 'Stern Nurse of Men'. This first encounter and irreverent brush with authority was the rooting of a long and deep friendship. Dave Venters and I had many things in common.

Academic prowess carried little weight among one's companions. In the country of the schoolboy, the games player is king. I see no reason to deplore this indisputable fact. I had moved from the domain of a former Rugby captain of England to the care and tutelage of a former captain of Scotland, the great J.H. Bruce Lockhart, both my Housemaster and Headmaster. That he was also a cosummate musician and water-colour artist impressed me enormously. Rugger, unlike soccer, did not call, at my level, for tremendous technical skill, and I managed not to disgrace myself, principally because I was far too much of a coward ever to run the risk of being accused of cowardice. My friend Dave, however, was a natural games player of considerable promise. This apart, we shared music, art, singing (he bass and I tenor, which promoted harmony rather than rivalry), a love of drama and a finely attuned sense of the ridiculous which was constantly to land us both in trouble.

He who does not excel on the games field must work that much harder to gain acceptance among his peers. Such forced application can pay dividends in later life when the sporting hero, his capital spent, is reduced to beery reunions at Twickenham to ape an ancient rage and nostalgic post-prandial illustration of old strategies with the aid of empty wine glasses and the cruet. Brains were discounted, though an occasional crib for a Latin unseen could curry favour with some sinewy demi-god ('Put in a few mistakes or he'll know it's not mine!'). Wealth was also disregarded, but having a pretty sister could do wonders for a chap's popularity. The scientist came into his own if he happened to have a sound working knowledge of the internal combustion engine. Music was important to those who taught us (it was rumoured that to qualify as a master an applicant had to play either international rugger or an orchestral instrument) but of little value in vulgar currency unless you happened to be adept at the jazz trumpet. The role I developed was that of wit and wag. With ears and eyes ever alert for humour in a situation, I survived like Jack Point and laughed at myself till I ached for it.

On our first afternoon we climbed Winder. Sedbergh is surrounded by hills and mountains, all with their distinct personalities as is the nature of hills and mountains. Winder, although neither the highest nor the most difficult, is close by, rising steeply to over fifteen hundred feet, and dominates school and town. I was to reach the cairns of all the hills in the course of the next five years – by no means always by choice, as fell running was an integral part of school discipline – but this familiar massif was my first experience of anything approaching a mountain. The face, covered blandly with turf close-cropped by sheep, was corregated by narrow runnels where generations of boys, the summit reached, would ski down balanced on one heel at awesome speed. The gradient and breadth of this tilted plateau produced a dreamlike illusion. Wide enough to fill the field of vision to the periphery, it insisted that you and your companions were pushing yourselves along a limitless flat plain, leaning precariously forward, and, as when escaping some peril in a nightmare, scarcely able to move your leaden limbs.

Climbing Winder had once been a frequent punishment for misdemeanour, as the culprits could be watched throughout in comfort from the cricket field below. On this occasion, as so long before on introduction to a new school, I found a colony of Fox moth caterpillars. I had no tin with me and pushed them optimistically into a back pocket of my shorts. I got them back to the House and transferred them to a makeshift breeding cage unscathed. At least the caterpillars were happy enough; I had a persistent nettle rash on my backside from their hairy presence for the ensuing week.

The uncomprisingly rural character of our environment has left its mark on every boy who passed through the school from its founding in 1525 to the present day. Eton brands its progeny with an air of urbane sophistication; Winchester imparts a slightly self-effacing aura of good manners (as its founder would have wished); and other establishments all leave their own recognizable stamps. My House Tutor of those days, later to become Headmaster and a personal friend, described the typical Old Sedberghian as a Hard Boiled Ham with Hair growing out of his Ears. This is often near enough the truth to be piercingly funny, but on the whole, though in no way an ingénue, the Sedbergh boy emerges with a kind of unselfconscious innocence.

Sedbergh is at least ten miles from anywhere, and urban temptations were far removed. The neighbouring towns of Kendal and Kirkby Lonsdale, hardly renowned for fleshpots anyway, are just within this radius but well out of reach. As we were able to travel only where our feet could carry us and get back in time for tea, there were no statutory 'bounds' and apart from the little town itself, accessible with a signed leave for shopping, and the miniscule hamlet of Millthrop, where TB was reputed to lurk, we could go anywhere. On a line due north, incredibly, no town lies between Sedbergh and the Bass Rock two hundred miles away.

Thus isolated, like the nearby land-locked lakes, the school and the town had evolved together for centuries. There was no constraint of 'them and us' or 'town and gown' rivalry. Identification was ensured by the school uniform. Early in his career as Headmaster, Bruce Lockhart had devised 'The Blues'. Except on Sundays, when the rig was suits or sports jackets (half the school wore the kilt), we wore an ensemble of navy blue blazers, shorts and stockings, and wore open-neck shirts regardless of the weather. In a more worldly milieu this would have been open to ridicule; as it was, especially as clothes rationing was still in operation, it was inexpensive and extremely practical. School Prefects were privileged to wear the blazer open and to carry an umbrella. As the annual rainfall was some five feet, the latter was more than a mere badge of rank. A first-termer was permitted one hand in one jacket pocket — he had to alternate from left to right to keep the circulation going. Available pockets increased as the year progressed, and the fourth term saw a seasoned veteran who could thrust hands into pockets at will and had finished his days of fagging.

Life, viewed from a distance of more than half a lifetime in the comfort of the central heating and a relatively unfettered autonomy, was certainly tough. Far from breaking the spirit, it strengthened and supplemented it, though it would be false to pretend I nurse any longing to return to such ascetic monasticism today. The dawn runs so often attributed to the school never took place, and I doubt if any vainglorious raconteur ever claimed that they did. None the less, to the frequent comments, 'Sedbergh? Isn't that the place where you run up hills before breakfast?', one would merely reply in the affirmative rather than launch into tedious detail.

The old clichés are, like a dog's bad name, notoriously hard to live down. In vain would J.H. Bruce Lockhart reiterate on Speech Days that the principal aims of the school were worship of God, scholarship, music and Rugby Football in that order. The press would as persistently publish the headline, 'Rugby Football principal aim of Sedbergh School, states Headmaster'. The only pre-breakfast imposition was early prep at twenty past seven. This was a hardship until you were promoted to a study, whereafter it was just a question of transferring your comatose form from bed to cold bath to makeshift couch.

Cold baths were mandatory every morning, but as it was a lightning in and out ('Get your shoulders under!') it held no terrors for a habitué of the Malsis plunge. There were two bathrooms in School House, an upper and a lower, floored with duckboards and each containing two massive Victorian tubs which could comfortably have housed a pair of hippos. Cast in glazed earthenware, they had stout wooden surrounds, treacherous when slippery with soap. One was filled with cold water every morning. Into the other you emptied the contents of the basin from your washstand from the night before. The long dormitories, divided by wooden partitions into cubicles for privacy, were ventilated either side by a row of big square windows which pivoted to the horizontal and stood wide every night. Thus open to the weather it was not uncommon in winter, when blankets were augmented with rugs and greatcoats, to find on waking a couple of inches of snow on the foot of the bed. A familiar sight on shivering along to the cold bath on freezing winter mornings was the other tub piled high with lumps of ice like petrified puddings, tipped from the moulds of the overnight basins.

Cold baths are now a relic of the past. This defection caused some comment from the Hard Boiled Hams. It has often been my lot in life to find myself the central character of a Bateman cartoon. You know the sort of thing – a large, detailed drawing shows the guests at a crowded banquet all staring with irate indignation at one embarrassed little fellow, and the caption reads: 'The Man who Drank the Water from his Finger Bowl'. At a reunion dinner, the Demise of the Cold Bath was being far from coldly discussed. The wine was excellent, or mischief might not have claimed me so easily as an ally, but I asked in a loud voice, 'You don't really think cold baths are character forming?' The apoplectic chorus of unleashed snorts would not have disgraced a herd of angry bison. The cowed devil's advocate stared innocently at his plate. For the record, I rather think they are.

Although lessons, assemblies and general school activities took place in a cluster of large school buildings, domestic and extra-curricular life centred round the House. There were seven of them, in and around the town, separate units, each housing some fifty boys, run largely by the prefects with the guidance of a resident House Tutor and presided over by a Housemaster who lived in guessed-at splendour behind a green baize door. Dad had placed me, Tim and Patrick in different houses, with different customs and different loyalties, so that we hardly met except by prior arrangement, and in many ways we could well have been in different schools. Tim sat successfully for a scholarship the year following my arrival and joined me in the September. In the main, we mutually agreed, our separation within the system was a satisfactory set-up, and it probably did much to maintain our close friendship in the holidays.

The Christmas and Lent terms, with the exception of Sundays and, in unusually fine weather, the occasional extra half-holiday, gave little scope for free-range activity. Afternoons were spent either on the rugger field (the round ball was strictly taboo) or on a run: three miles on a full school day, seven miles on a half-holiday. Even the booking of a fives or squash court involved a compulsory short run before or after the game. Runs provided a useful familiarity with the locality, its routes and footpaths, but no chances to explore in detail. It rained, more or less continuously, from September to March, with frost and snow as a respite early in the year. When, as happened with annual consistency in my schooldays, the frosts were keen enough to congeal tarn and stream, regular exercise gave place to idyllic days of skating.

When the playing fields became too hard for sport, Dave and I used to climb a nearby fell to a small tarn, always the first to freeze over, where there was time for a brief half-hour on the ice before we had to leave for the return journey. With luck a week later the news would come that Lilymere was bearing. Lilymere was a privately owned lake in the hills to the west of us, set among heather and pine trees and stretching about a mile in its longest extent. The school was invited whenever the ice had reached a safe thickness, and we would pile into buses, in a motley of eccentric sports gear which accentuated the jubilant lapse from routine.

I can conjure yet the sweet, cold air rushing past, the taste of resin and snow, the crisp hiss of skates on new ice, the muffled cries and laughter and that round, hollow throbbing to which the very viscera thrilled, the growls of the living ice. With a kind of pain I often gazed at the moorland and the pines as the sun moved low, sharp silhouettes against snow as pink as blancmange, and understood that some scenes could not be put on to canvas. Painted with truth, they would be too vulnerable to the cynic's charge of blatant chocolate-box sentimentality.

Skating weather was lit by limpid, cloudless skies, when the air itself seemed to crackle. Back at school a hollow saucer in the fields had been flooded and aptly christened the Bruce Loch, near enough for skating in breaks and short periods of freedom. From here one morning I witnessed with friends three suns in the sky, some rare phenomenon doubtless caused by ice crystals suspended way up in the empyrean, but fraught all the same with unscientific feelings about awful portents and the Day of Judgement. The aurora was always visible at night during these spells: shifting, flickering columns of pale colour reaching upwards into limitless vastness. It made the affairs and schemes of men seem very small. Such keen weather never lasted long, two to three weeks at the most. For the rest of the year the Bruce Loch reverted to a man-made dewpond, a guardian noticeboard bearing the forlorn command, 'Do not throw stones on the ice.'

In contrast the summer term was a tranquil season. My time was more my own, and my excursions into the wild were self-imposed. Ring ousels nested on the lower slopes of Winder – mountain blackbirds with white waistcoats but giving the typical blackbird alarm calls when disturbed and singing from the rocks above the nest like their garden cousins. Some four miles to the north-east, under the bulk of The Calf, reared the black ramparts of Cautley Crag, a crescent scar of vertical cliffs on which the sun has never shone. Here the ravens nested. Their twiggy platform was inaccessible on a stunted birch growing precariously out from the rock face. Ravens lay their eggs betimes, in January or early February, and the family would be well established by the time I was able to visit them with any regularity. By April, buzzards and peregrine falcons would have joined the nesting community at Cautley.

Baugh Fell, a wide, flat table mountain, closed the valleys to the east. At certain times the fell is encircled, in the fashion of table mountains, by a helm wind which blows around the circumference of the fell just below the flat summit. A level collar of cloud proclaims the helm wind to the valley below. Around the pools and peat bogs of the spongy table-top nested the pretty little dunlin, smallest of our commoner waders, conspicuous by their chestnut backs and black tummies. Running over the humps and tussocks like clockwork toys, they would take to the air and ascend like skylarks in a hovering spiral, trilling and piping, or chase each other, jinking and twisting at speed over the white tufts of bog cotton.

My grandfather had been a keen amateur photographer, and with one of his old cameras, a 'Carbide' quarter-plate, I would spend hours in a home-made hide photographing birds on the nest. Here I had the assistance of a friend and ally, D.P. Guild, known, predictably, as 'Dippy'. He was more photographer than ornithologist, but had one surprising ability. Owing to a slight red-green colour blindness, he was unerringly quick at spotting the camouflaged eggs of curlew or lapwing lying in their scrapes on the rough ground – in spite of being short-sighted. Even more impressive was the distance at which he could pick out the caterpillars of the Emperor moth on gorse or heather. These caterpillars, a stout three inches when full grown, are a bright emerald with black spines surrounding raised yellow or pink pimples. Gaudy, one might think, but on the food-plant they are inconspicuous and take some finding. Dippy could detect them a good ten yards away.

I had converted my hide from an old striped awning. It looked incongruously like an old-fashioned bathing tent stuck in the middle of the moor. Our favourite site was the nearby rise of Frost Row, which provided a variety of habitat: marsh, reeds, heather, scrub and bare scree. We would choose a suitable nest, for instance a curlew's, with four olive eggs, lug up the heavy hide and erect it thirty yards away. At this distance the birds took little notice of it but returned fairly quickly to the nest.

By halving the distance each day, we would move the hide up towards the nest and would retire to a vantage point with our binoculars to mark the reappearance of the disturbed bird. In five days we would have got close enough to set up the camera. Any reeds or grass which obstructed the view of the nest would have been carefully removed, a little at a time, over the approach period. At the same time two large safety pins had been stuck close together near the hole where the lens would protrude. This accustomed the bird to sporadic clicks as the wind blew. The sudden noise of a camera shutter could otherwise create alarm.

Birds cannot count accurately beyond two, but they are not fooled without some subterfuge. If we were lucky we might bribe a handful of friends to 'put us in the hide' – that is, wait until we were installed, then continue on their way; but more often we enlisted the aid of an old hat and a macintosh. One of us would scramble quickly into the hide, the other would hold the mac at arm's length, the hat above it, and disappear over the hill talking loudly to this makeshift companion. The ruse was employed in reverse to extricate the cramped photographer some time later.

Such intimate eavesdropping on a bird in its natural setting brought many moments of intense joy and often much humour. It was a rare privilege to experience the conversation of a hen lapwing, quietly calling her mate as he stood guard and answered her from a nearby hill top. The calls we hear in the general run are too often warning notes or danger signals. A building pair of yellow wagtails rocked us with suppressed laughter as, tiring of the search for hair to line the nest, they hit on the idea of getting it straight from a cow which was relaxing conveniently close. You could feel the 'ping' as each separate hair was tugged out and the bird scuttered backward to escape the flicking tail.

There was the curlew, obstinately sticking to her nest while pecking indignantly with her long bill at the black face of an encroaching ewe, grazing too close for comfort. Her exasperation at the stupidity of the placid invader, which she managed to repel, was infectious. The most galling lesson was provided by a pair of wheatears. Though Fox moth caterpillars were often plentiful at the end of the year, they are notoriously difficult to rear safely through the winter. They wait until the following spring to spin up and complete their life cycle. Thus I had only two reared specimens and never found the moth in the open. The wheatears, feeding their chicks under a limestone rock, brought them an almost exclusive diet of Fox moths, captive and fluttering, and would emerge from the nest hole to drop, with exquisite mockery, four inert fulvous-brown wings after every snack.

One afternoon on the River Lune I was busy on a water-colour of Middleton Bridge when I became aware that I was sharing the shingle bank with a nesting oyster-catcher. The sunny spot and the contrasting pied plumage of the bird (they have feet and bill as red as sealing wax, but colour photography was not then the province of the amateur) convinced me that this would be a promising site for some photography from the hide. The catch was that it was rather a long way out, and the tackle, still up on Frost Row, was cumbersome, as we knew too well. Dippy, with sudden inspiration, suggested we should ask a certain retired major if we might borrow his donkey and cart. This we duly did, loaded the hide and set off with the reluctant moke.

The journey took far longer than the five miles warranted, nevertheless we set up the hide. On the return journey the donkey switched from his mood of state funeral to one straight out of *Ben Hur*, and we rollicked home at breakneck speed, hind hooves drumming on the front of the cart as we clung on. The oyster-catcher, by contrast, proved to be the most complacent subject. The nesting bird had two positions as it slept. In one, the bill was neatly tucked backwards into its plumage, pointing south. The other position was identical, only pointing north. Fortunately, after an hour of slumber, its mate would arrive. They would spend a few minutes in an impressive courtship display, allowing one good photograph of the pair, then the other bird would take its place on the nest and the scene would revert to its customary somnolence.

Not long afterwards I found myself fostering a trio of baby tawny owls. These fluffy youngsters hatch at staggered intervals, so they always come in diminishing sizes like the three bears. These waifs had been blown out of an old magpie nest, and I found them in a deserted farmyard under a rusting chain harrow. I put them in straw in a disused calf pen, protected by a low wall, and called daily with raw meat. The second day I discovered they were not orphans. High in a sycamore sat Mum, motionless, staring at me with half-lidded eyes.

Each day I came to feed them until first the largest, then the second baby stared down at me alongside the parent in the sycamore tree.

Finally they were gone and the tree was empty. The interesting aspect of this happy collaboration was that the parent (I only ever saw one adult during the day), far from resenting my intrusion, fed them every night. Furthermore, she left a supply for the following day laid neatly on the little wall top: mostly voles and fieldmice, but also frogs and, unexpectedly, fish. These latter were the little fish known as bullheads, or miller's thumbs, from the nearby beck. In one old reference book – I found no mention of it in contemporary ones – it was stated that 'the tawny owl is reputed to catch fish'. I can endorse that reputation, for I know the tawny owl catches fish – and feeds its family on them.

Beyond Frost Row, up the valley of the little River Dee, sat the village of Dent. Though now a site for coach tours and cottage industry and in danger of becoming a bit folksy, Dent was then a rustic ghost of its former glory as centre of the wool carding trade, unvisited and isolated. 'We're short of nowt we've got,' was a recurrent saying of my grandfather, 'and if there's owt we've not got, we'll do as they do in Dent!' What do they do in Dent? They go baht! Which is Yorkshire for going without, as in 'baht 'at'. Dent was even seven miles away from Dent Station, on the Settle–Carlisle railway, so replenishing stocks of anything was clearly a historic problem.

The touring coaches are still debarred from the centre of Dent, owing to its compact maze of narrow cobbled streets and little stone cottages. In the market-place still stands a hefty obelisk of Shap granite, memorial to Adam Sedgwick, one-time pupil and master at Sedbergh, the father of modern geology. As a professor at Cambridge he was instrumental in sending his protégé, Charles Darwin, on his momentous voyage in *The Beagle*, which also places him as godfather of the modern theory of evolution. He was born in Dent vicarage.

The square little church is paved with Dent marble. This is not a true marble, but a sedimentary limestone quarried from an adjacent scar. The stone is crammed with white fossils in a dark grey matrix and, when polished smooth, presents a streaked appearance very like marble. The more fossils, the paler the stone, whereas the sparser pieces are darker. Contrasting squares were chosen to pave the aisle and altar steps like a chessboard. The fossils in their polished tombs display their every detail, sections from every plane. I would fancy the young Adam, bored by his father's long address, indulging in his first fascinating studies in palaeontology by examining the floor at his feet. On the other hand, the stones may not have been there in his boyhood, and were perhaps laid at his suggestion.

One extra half-holiday, Dave and I had climbed over Rise Hill to spend a happy afternoon painting on the broad flank of Whernside. The day deteriorated and, chilled and a little damp, we dropped down into Dent and enquired at the Rising Sun if there was any chance of a hot meal. The landlord's wife, an ample lady in a long apron, said ruefully, 'Nay, I can't give you anything hot.' Seeing our crestfallen reaction, she added, 'But I've a bit of ham.' We sat down in the tiny bar parlour in front of a friendly fire – we rarely saw a fire in the term time – and thawed out. After a while our hostess came back with two enormous plates, both hidden by overlapping slabs of grilled home-cured ham, crisp and still sizzling, topped by three fried eggs. This was supplemented by a mound of home-baked bread and butter and a pot of tea so strong you could have trotted a mouse on it. We wondered, after working steadily away in silence for many minutes, what she thought we had meant by a hot meal. I think it cost us half-a-crown for the lot.

6

Of Music,
Masters and Men

Emperor moths

I AN HAY DESCRIBED SCHOOLMASTERING AS, 'THE MOST RESPONSIBLE, the least advertised, the worst paid and the most richly rewarded profession in the world'. Certainly no profession is richer in memorable characters, principally because one meets them at the most impressionable age. As important as the study of what you were taught, if not more so, was the study of the idiosyncrasies and temperaments of those who taught you. Perennially you hear that, in life as in the classroom, there aren't the old characters about that there used to be. Be reassured, but at the same time be wary. The sense of character, like the senses of taste and smell, fades imperceptibly as life passes, and only strong flavours continue to excite the palate. You are unaware that your contemporaries have surely replaced the old characters, and even blinder to the fact that, in truth, you may have become one yourself.

The art master, Sandy Inglis, a red-bearded Scot with a twinkling eye, naturally had a considerable influence on Tim, Dave and myself as we spent much of our spare time in the art school. We would see him cycling off on free days in deerstalker and knickerbockers, easel and canvas strapped on the step, like a character out of *Trilby*. His style was more modern than that of Du Maurier's heroes, though he had the good teacher's ability to encourage without imprinting his own manner or opinions on his pupils. Early in my career he told me dourly, 'You draw pretty well. When we've taught you how to paint you might make something of yourself.' A more lasting Inglis aphorism still gives me comfort today. 'It don't matter so much what you do, or even how well you do it; it's having the damn cheek to do it at all that counts!'

Inevitably, however, pupil will imitate master. As patterns I had the conventional landscapes and classical values of Bruce Lockhart on one side of the scale and the cubist technique and mild iconoclasm of Inglis on the other and, biased as it might be by Munnings to the right and Matisse the left, I achieved a sort of balance. The company in the art school had radical tendencies. Though rebellion was never seriously contemplated, we fancied ourselves in the role of philosopher and critic. In those days we were housed upstairs in the original sixteenth-century school building, in a friendly, cluttered atelier later converted into a splendid library by Brendan Bracken. A well-equipped modern art school was duly built, and I helped to inaugurate it, but it lacked the comfortable informality of the old loft.

Painting and drawing and the plastic arts, though occupying one part of the mind absorbedly, leave the tongue free to wag. The young John Arden, whose talents were not long afterwards to manifest themselves in writer and playwright, was undisputed leader of the group of quasi-dissidents, satirically fluent and usually waspishly funny. He spent much of his time designing stage sets and period costume for Molière or Restoration drama in painstaking and colourful detail. He was, incidentally, the first Hamlet I ever saw, full of sound and fury and, to my tender years, remarkably good. To my surprise and disappointment, considering his bright designs, the production was costumed in modern (the 1940s were modern) dress – mostly evening dress.

The Reverend Austin Timotheus Isaiah Boggis taught me with infinite patience to play the oboe. I had had leanings towards the bassoon, but as there was already a competent bassoonist in the House Orchestra and a vacancy for a second oboe, I was persuaded to adopt my second choice, less flamboyant but more lyrical. Most choices in all spheres were House oriented. To be honest, nothing lyrical, or remotely tuneful, emerged from my instrument for a couple of years. The oboe is a frustrating instrument for the beginner. I collected records of Leon Goossens and Evelyn Rothwell, so I knew what I wanted to sound like. They made it seem so easy.

When I practised at home our dachshund, the unsaintly Paul, would sit outside the door, muzzle pointing heavenward, and howl balefully in agonized accompaniment. I maintained that he simply did not appreciate music. Tim and Patrick reckoned that the trouble was he did. People are forever attributing mistaken traits to their pets. I remember the three of us, one wintry day on the Eastbourne shore, meeting a lady throwing a stick into the waves while her black labrador looked on with incurious patience. 'Oh, he's such a stupid dog!' she exclaimed testily. 'He'll never bring it back!' We told her we thought he showed sound judgement and intelligence; the sea looked far from inviting, and he knew that if he retrieved the stick she'd only throw the blessed thing straight back in again.

Atti-B, to give the Reverend Boggis his less respectful but more manageable title, at our first meeting examined my lips and teeth as one would those of a carthorse before purchasing, elicited that I could hold a tin whistle, casually handed to me, and, when my fingers instinctively covered the right holes, pronounced that I might be able to make a go of the oboe. This was my entrée into a world which was to give me immense pleasure, many friends and not a few adventures in the years to come. Anglican in calling, the Reverend

Boggis was wholly catholic as a musician. He claimed he could not play the clarinet, but I doubted this. Organist and pianist, he played every other orchestral instrument. The viola he played clasped between his knees, because, as he said, he had been taught to play the 'cello but never the violin. I suspect that, under the chin, it would have collided with his dog-collar. I was always welcome to borrow a book from his extensive library, and he was knowledgeable about butterflies. He envied me my Large Tortoiseshell which he saw on the setting board.

The rarest commodity of schooldays was privacy, especially in the winter and spring terms. Not that I was a loner or a young Shelley, flitting from the company of his fellows like a hunted fawn, but there are times when a chap likes a few minutes to himself. The chapel was never locked, and it was here that I would find sanctuary in the half-light when the crowd proved too madding. Peace comes in many guises, not all of them silent. From a back pew I would often listen undiscovered to an impromptu organ recital from our Musical Director, lost in fugue and canon, in all likelihood escaping from the turmoil as I was. Bach's D Minor Toccata and Fugue summoned every nuance from the chapel organ, and seemed to emanate from the very stones of the austere building. That exciting bass growl from the biggest pipe, which gathers up the first phrases and flings them up in a triumphant paeon, gave no sound. Rather every flagstone of the floor seemed to shake.

Chapel, of course, was normally a communal institution, combining, twice every Sunday, religious observance with visible reminders of rank and hierarchy; that fusion of the spiritual and the secular common to proud cathedral and village church alike down the ages. For the first, the worship was simple and sincere. For the second, the proletariat sat in order of caste and degree, as they still do, the choir in lofty detachment. The school prefects make stately entry, two by two, resplendent with floral buttonholes. The masters, capped and gowned, take descending places alongside the aisle; the Headmaster, in surplice and hood, moves in solitary dignity to his pew below the choir stalls; God's in his Heaven, all's right with the world.

That memorable headmaster Dr Keat, in his inaugural address to the boys of Eton, thundered from the pulpit, 'Boys, be pure in heart! For if you're not I'll flog you till you are!' Bruce Lockhart's sermons were gentler in texture, rich Celtic poetry culled from wild skies and highland torrents and the morning stars singing together, though I recall him on one occasion, after dwelling on the great men who had climbed great mountains, reflecting with the suspicion of a twinkle in his Scots eye that, 'there are little hills for little men; and they are condemned if they are too indolent to scramble to the top.'

Visiting preachers gave promise of a change of routine on Sunday evenings, but it is inevitably the eccentrics who remain in my memory. These we had in plenty, from the stylish performances of Bryan Green, soi-disant Vicar of Birmingham, who would rock his congregation with gales of laughter, to the fireworks of Knox-like ministers of the Kirk, who, fists hammering the pulpit, would cow it with terror. 'And the people cry up from the bottomless pit, "We didna ken, Laird, we didna ken!" And the good Laird looks down in his infinite mercy, and says, "Well! Ye ken the noo!"'

Bishop Gorton of Coventry climbed the steps to the pulpit on a hot summer evening. The chapel doors stood wide, letting in shafts of sunlight, and a cooling little breeze eddied round, enticing us to get outside and get on with life. As if to emphasize the point, it lifted the preacher's notes and scattered them, oscillating gently, to the floor below. 'That's all I had to say,' announced the magnificent Gorty. 'It wasn't worth saying anyway. And now to God the Father . . .' It was the shortest sermon I can remember, and, if brevity be the soul of wit, the wittiest.

One sonorous Scot, whose name and rank I forget, treated us to a litany almost rivalling the Benedicite, exhorting as it does every beast, bird and plant to bless the Lord through a few hundred verses. 'The rain,' he asked in rhetorical gloom, 'whence cometh it? From below? No! From above! The sunshine, whence cometh it? From below? No! From above!' This continued in the same repetitive vein interminably through hail and harvest, starlight and storm, the standard answer increasing in volume each time to a deafening crescendo. Finally he boomed 'Man, whence cometh he? From below?' We all roared, to a man, 'NO! FROM ABOVE!' Whether or not this was his intended finale, it stopped him in his tracks. We felt he had made his point.

Father Horner used to come and conduct a short voluntary service every Wenesday evening in Lent. Elderly, puckish, a tiny little figure in a monk's robe, he was superior of an order near the poorer quarters of Bradford and was an eager Rugby League enthusiast. He was the only saint I have ever met, though he would have deprecated the notion. One misty evening as he stood in the pulpit I saw a halo round his grey head, like the nimbus round each altar candle. His message was one of tranquillity. 'Be still, and know that I am God,' he would command quietly. I have not found such stillness since.

Sundays in the winter terms had, apart from matins and evensong, a rather negative quality, a hangover from the days when work on the sabbath, even moving a chair across a room, was considered a sin. It was no doubt a salutary scheme that the life of a schoolboy should have been so organized and timetabled from waking to sleeping on all other days, but, as the old adage puts it, it is the hands that have not learnt to be idle for which the devil finds some mischief still. I have spent my life learning to be idle. I think I have a natural gift for it. Enforced idleness, nevertheless, puts a strain upon the spirit, and Sundays, when one was turned out of the House for the afternoon, come rain or shine, without organized activity, presented an unwelcome limbo.

Down on Millthrop Bridge, scene on sunnier days of sketching and fly-fishing, a remarkable orator would proclaim the second coming on blustery Sunday afternoons. George Paley, shell-shocked from the Great War, wild of eye and wilder of garb in a tattered macintosh, flat cap and a long woollen scarf flying in the wind, would once a week harangue the world impartially for its sins, convinced he was the Messiah. That was indeed the name by which we knew him. As in later years I would in idle moments join the crowd round the Reverend Donald Soper on Tower Hill, I would listen to our local prophet, as he brandished his letters to the King and Mr Churchill (though never, I recall, their replies) and fielded the gibes of the hooting barrackers with fiery scorn. If his message was garbled and illogical, his sincerity was startling and I felt his disturbing pathos with a helpless insight.

Another veteran of the trenches was our House boiler-and-handyman, Mr Peck, a wiry gnome, wizened and desiccated. Ingenuous new boys would be persuaded to address him as 'Peck'. He would turn with furious energy. 'I've got an 'andle to me name!' Such disrespect was never repeated. Mr Peck rang the rising bell every morning with malevolent enjoyment. Stumping irascibly into the common room – even his arthritis was an indictment – he would dump our post on the window sill and examine each letter in turn, holding the envelope up within a couple of inches of his tobacco-blind eyes, livid duck-egg irises with pin-point pupils. His blindness was curiously spasmodic. Half-way across the room he would fix his gaze on a table top. Striding over and pointing with unerring accuracy, he would rasp, 'That scratch wasn't there yesterday!'

Though Mr Peck was quite impartial in his ill disposition towards the world in general, the prefect for whom I was private fag in my early days, one Dick Sanderson, treated him almost with camaraderie. He was Captain of House Rugger, a fast centre on the School XV, and was later to win an MC in Korea, so he was clearly a man of derring-do, but even so his courage was impressive. One day in expansive and indulgent mood he took me down the dungeon steps of the boiler house to watch his friend Mr Peck shaving. Remembering the elaborate ritual of my grandfather, I was astounded to see the other face, as it were, of the operation. Here again was a cut-throat razor, but an ancient weapon, chipped and scarred. Mr Peck pulled a potato out of his pocket, used the venerable instrument to saw a slice off it, and rubbed it vigorously all over his face. Peering into a shard of spotted mirror, he scraped away assiduously in the dimness.

My father told me how, when a boy, he had been 'beating' for pocket money on the Bolton Abbey grouse moors, and was summoned during the lunch break in great secrecy by the keeper, an old family friend. Crawling on their tummies through the rough, they reached the lip of a little hollow. The keeper pointed. 'See tha! Over there!' There, discreetly hidden, stood their Sovereign, having a pee in the heather. It was a signal honour, conferred by the keeper on very few, and left, my father claimed, a lasting affection for the Monarchy. In lesser degree my experience was similar. Many Old Sedberghians have risen to important heights in Church and State, but very few watched Mr Peck shaving.

The boiler house has one other claim to a place in my memory, for it was on its stone entrance that I found a specimen of the Grey Mountain Carpet moth. This is one of the instances which cause the uninitiated to question the sanity of the moth collector, for the Grey Mountain Carpet is no bright beauty and its wing-tips don't even span the letters of its name. In the same way, I would look at a prized stamp in the collection of a friend and wonder in my ignorance why it should be valued above so many more colourful specimens elsewhere in the album, much as a child would prefer a bright new florin to a grubby old ten shilling note. I explained to the scoffers that this was the first truly northern species I had come across. There is a very large family of Carpet moths, a few hundred of them. They don't eat your carpets. The name is derived from the intricate eastern carpet patterns on the wings. Next time you see one of these frail little moths on your window pane, butterfly-like in their delicacy, spare five minutes to look closely, with a magnifying glass if you have one to hand. What at first seems a dull grey insect will reveal its beauty in an infinite symmetrical mosaic. Beware, though, if your life be a busy one, for, once tasted, the experience can be habit-forming.

I had many productive forays on the fells with the net. The Ruby Tiger flew on the moorland heather at great speed, a stocky little moth with rounded brown forewings contrasting with pale, lilac blue hindwings, a flash of ruby fanning on to them from a bright red body. The colours merged in flight to a brownish bullet, and only in the net did you discover what you had caught.

Most moorland moths fly at speed. No doubt the terrain demands this, as, once above the heather, there is no cover. A little gem, easily overlooked, was the Beautiful Yellow Underwing, fairly plentiful on sunny afternoons in May and June. It has a wingspan of a mere three-quarters of an inch, the forewings a patchwork of crimson, grey and white above golden yellow hindwings bordered with a broad black band. Surprisingly, as it sits on the tip of a heather sprig it is difficult to spot, the broken patterns blending perfectly with the early buds of the flower.

The aristocrat of the heather is the Emperor moth. Large and furry, of all our 'eyed' species its four painted eyes are the most startling, principally because the eye on each forewing is surrounded by an oval 'white', increasing the staring deception. The male is purplish grey with an orange tinge to the hindwings, curvily waved and banded with black and rose-pink with a scalloped white border. His Empress is larger still, her wings similarly marked on a dove grey background. I have already described the caterpillars, but the cocoon of this remarkable moth deserves some mention. Flask-shaped, ginger brown with a coarse texture like coconut matting, it is spun among the twigs of the gorse or heather. It is a tough structure, and the narrow end of the flask is sealed with a fibrous trapdoor like the entrance to a lobster pot in reverse. The fibres of the trap bend easily to let the moth out on hatching, but stiffly resist any intruder from outside. Once the trap shuts again after emergence, only the light weight betrays the fact that the moth has left its cocoon.

The male Emperors flew strongly over the heather on Baugh Fell and Frost Row, and the hunt was an unequal one, pursuit hampered by the springy growth, often waist high. A moth hurrying in your direction would become aware of you when some five yards away and then the frantic chase was on, usually to end in pursuer sprawled and scratched face down in the engulfing scrub, a cock grouse testily rebuking you to 'Go back! Go back! Go back!' Guile was required to catch the Emperor in relative comfort.

If one was lucky enough to have bred a recently emerged female, the game took a different course. For the Emperor is one of a handful of moths, mostly large and frequenting broad spaces of heath or moorland, who succumb readily to a trick of the collector known in the trade as 'assembling'. The female emits a scent which is carried long distances on the breeze. The males are sensitive to incredibly dilute concentrations of this scent. Picking up a trace during his hasty patrolling of the moor, a male will change course and home in on the strengthening scent. I don't think the functions of the antennae, the slender horns of butterfly and moth, are fully understood, but I observed that those of the 'assembling' moths, including the Emperors, have a common structure. Those of the female are narrow filaments and relatively short, but the antennae of the male form thick, fringed combs. Take a virgin Empress up to the heather on a sunny May afternoon, her box secured with muslin, and the males will come from miles away and sit round the edge with their tongues hanging out. Often the first indication that an Empress or Oak Eggar has hatched in the breeding cage is an enthusiastic male flapping noisily at the window to be let in.

I reared two caterpillars of a closely related moth, the lovely Kentish Glory, found on sallow in a wood near my Sussex home, and they hatched out in my study in the June of 1952. Both of these fairly rare moths were females – sadly, as I was hoping to raise a family. The Kentish Glory also responds to the assembling technique and I found it had been taken in Yorkshire, though not very often. (Sedbergh was then firmly in Yorkshire, though it has since been treacherously seceded to Cumbria by governmental decree.) I duly spent lazy hours sunbathing on the squash court roof, my two nubile beauties alongside, but alas no errant male responded to the call and my random matchmaking was to no avail.

I found a supportive ally in my obsession with natural history in the stately person of Mrs Bruce Lockhart. The Housemaster's wife traditionally assumed the role either of housekeeper or of house matron. Mrs Bruce Lockhart chose the latter, attending to minor ailments, cuts and bruises (half the school at any given time had some appendage in plaster), while anything of a more serious nature was referred to the sanatorium. 'Mrs Bruce Lockhart' was a mouthful to pronounce casually, even in rude health, usually emerging as a mumbled 'Mizbizzlewizzle'. (The great man's signature was even less decipherable. He once ruefully admitted receiving a letter directed to Mr J.H. Bumble Lumble.) I got to know her in my first year when I became a minor casualty. The constant running, on feet as flat as a duck's, had resulted in a crack in a metatarsal – what the Army called a 'march fracture'. Thus once a week she would take me in the car to Lancaster Infirmary for treatment. On the way we would talk, and sometimes we would stop and look at the waders on the Lune estuary – where I saw my first greenshank – or descend through the old water-mill at Killington to watch the return of the migrant salmon leaping the falls by the ancient salmon ladder. Thereafter I would be summoned whenever a maimed bird or an interesting moth presented itself.

In the last two years of my schooldays, ascending in the hierarchy, I sat at the top table of the House dining-room, presided over at lunchtime by the Bruce Lockharts. Lunch was never distinguished by haute cuisine, but the conversation, often I suspect cleverly steered, was stimulating. Visiting family friends and illustrious alumni attended the communal midday meal, to our naïve surprise, as they could surely lunch far more sumptuously elsewhere. Freda Bruce Lockhart, critic and broadcaster, and sister to the Headmaster, was a frequent visitor, as arthritic and frail as her reviews could be vigorous and implacable. Sir Robert, their brother, gave small clue in our eyes to the swashbuckling master-spy of his younger days; a Hannay grown humdrum, we thought, with the cruel insouciance of youth.

Our board was host to bishop and statesman, musician and scholar, names which I came later to recognize but which we then accepted without curiosity. My favourite regular was General Sir John Shea ('Jack to my friends, John to my brothers and sisters and Sir John to all Europe!'). A twinkling, dapper old warrior, wise and shrewd, he formed my picture of the Honourable Gally Threepwood in the Wodehouse saga of Blandings Castle. One morning as we waited reverently hushed for grace to be said, he turned stiffly in the silence and pronounced, 'Jolly good sausages, what?' Only he could have got away with it. On another occasion his monocle dropped abruptly into his soup. We waited expectantly, hoping he would lick it clean, but he merely fished it out and rubbed it in a handkerchief without interrupting the flow of his conversation.

Brendan Bracken stayed many times at his old House, roaming alone on the fells in shorts and sweater and a worn, peat-stained pair of plimsolls to get the London grime out of his lungs. It is in this attire that I immediately picture him, incongruous as it would have seemed to his colleagues at Westminster. The chief impression he conveyed was one of size. Any room seemed too small for him. A huge mane of pale, tawny hair, immensely thick lenses to his spectacles, the resounding hugeness of his voice, which even in relaxed conversation seemed to be addressing the other, wider House – these combined with an imposing frame to project an aura of latent power.

One Sunday Dave and I happened to be in the common room as Brendan passed through with a companion. Dave was wearing his native Sunday rig. 'Every Scot at Sedbergh should wear the kilt!' came the reverberating comment. 'This young man has the rump for it. Don't you agree, Pug?' The aptness of the name forced involuntary grins from Dave and myself, not unnoticed by the man so addressed whose square, blunt muzzle and sad eyes looked like nothing so much as a pedigree boxer dog. We had not recognized Lord Ismay, who, with Brendan, had in effect nursed Churchill through the dark days of the recent war.

In 1951 Patrick joined us at Sedbergh after nearly eight years at his prep school. I don't say Malsis were glad to move him on, but he had been there longer than most of the staff and it was felt he had no more to teach them. He took up the 'cello and prospered, on one occasion putting it down again so heavily that the old instrument, one Bertha, split, and a successor had to be found. This was the year of the Festival of Britain, and the school organized an extensive funfair on the playing fields as our contribution to the national jamboree. By general consent the most popular stall was devised and run by Patrick. On five separate tiles, five plastic grasshoppers were clamped flat by rubber suction cups fixed to their bellies. Springy wire legs splayed out, straining, and eventually freed the cup, causing the insect to jump vertically some four feet in the air. You paid a shilling for your grasshopper and stood to double your money if yours was the last to remain stuck down. The management won three bob every time. The stallholder's natural aptitude as entrepreneur, his busking patter and repartee brought him instant notoriety, and he was thoughtfully marked down as one who might need to be watched in the future.

In the February of 1952, returning to the House on a fittingly dismal day, hands thrust in trouser pockets with a pile of books under each arm and head pushed forward into the wind and rain, I was greeted with the solemn news that the King was dead. It must have been the unexpectedness that engraved the scene on my memory, for this was not the culmination of a long, publicized illness. Indeed, Princess Elizabeth and Prince Philip were away in Africa at the time, so the death of George VI must have been sudden. The wireless was still our medium, and it was with deep and reverent sorrow, many perched incongruously on window sills, tables and chair backs, that the House crowded in the common room to listen to the moving pomp of the great royal funeral.

Television was not to become widespread until just over a year later on the consequent royal occasion, this time one of joy in a young Queen and hope for the future. There was much typical academic quibbling from the Scottish element about the royal title. Although England's Elizabeth the Second, she was the first Elizabeth of Scotland and they wanted the point understood. How many thousands there must be who got their first television set for the coronation! A friend tells the story of taking a vanload of televisions that May up to the isolated little village of Lothersdale. Setting up the first, he asked the householder where he should plug it in. 'Plug it in? Nay, hell!' Lothersdale was not yet 'on the electric'.

Coronation Day fell on the second day of June in my final term at Sedbergh. That morning the news, delayed some five days, came though that Colonel John Hunt's expedition had been successful and that Hillary and Sherpa Tensing had at last stood on the summit of Everest. I had been taking a personal interest in the Everest attempt, because the official photographer was Tom Stobart, an old Malsis boy whose father had been a master at the school. The following is an extract from *The Times* of 10 July 1953:

> In London yesterday, Mr Stobart, a mountaineer as well as a cameraman, gave some account of his experiences. He kept a camera record up to Camp 5. At that height he slept with the cameras in his sleeping bag to keep them warm. He used an adapted ice pick as a tripod. At about 18,000 feet it became impossible to hold a camera sufficiently steady. He felt that in future expeditions the cameraman should be allowed some say in the colour of the expedition's apparel, for some of the climbers chose a blue that photographed ill against the background of snow. No films were taken at the summit, but a take by Stobart shows Hillary and Tensing returning to the main party to tell the story of their victory.

An earlier expedition was inspired in 1926 by a lantern lecture by Mr

N.E. Odell, a member of the 1924 Everest expedition. Note that Tom was not the cameraman. This account is adapted from *The Malsis Chronicle* of the time:

A TRIP TO EVEREST (BY US)

It took us some time to get everything together for the expedition. There were seven of us, all having different jobs; Turner was our pet naturalist and photographer (he hadn't a camera but that didn't matter). Stobart was the leader, carrying great boots; Swaine, sometimes called 'Horsie', was the porter and I was the oxygen manager. The oxygen, by the way, was water in bottles for drinking purposes. When we arrived at the bottom of the hill we roped ourselves together with the rope we had got and took up our sticks and started. When we had arrived at the top we ate all the grub except the skins and peel, which we carefully threw over the cliff to prevent a blot upon the gorgeous scenery, and returned by the path.

I was determined that Coronation Day should not prove a personal anti-climax. Several of my friends had gone with their parents to see the procession, and many more had gone home for the day for parties and the new wonder of the television set. General Sir John Shea had announced that he would stand outside the Admiralty in his Boy Scout Uniform – and indeed he did. My mother had sent me three little silk Union Jacks and, Everest dominant in my thoughts, I resolved to place one on each of the cairns of the famous Three Peaks of Yorkshire. Incidentally, I stepped out of a butcher's shop in Skipton the other day and met a woman with three pekes on a trifurcating lead. It was irresistible. 'Madam,' I said in congratulatory tone, 'Surely you call them Whernside, Ingleborough and Pen-y-Ghent?' She stared at me uncomprehendingly.

The weather was appalling, with pelting rain and heavy Yorkshire 'mizzle', and the round trip from Sedbergh was about thirty-five miles on foot. I set off at half past seven in the grey, sodden morning, was chased by a bull down Whernside, and lunched below at the Hill Inn on fresh salmon for two-and-threepence. I stuck the second flag on the cairn on Ingleborough to find a gaunt, black scarecrow figure like some medieval charcoal burner setting up a vast pile of car tyres for a beacon to be lit that evening. 'Where's Pen-y-Ghent?' I shouted in the wind and gloom, and he pointed a long arm without speaking. Taking, foolishly, the direct route, I found myself on the broad, fissured limestone pavement; impossible to maintain a stride, it was like running on railway sleepers.

On Pen-y-Ghent I sat below the cairn, in a scene worthy of Hitchcock, with a dead raven at my feet. Normally I would have carried it home to sketch, but I was too exhausted. I had done what I came to do. True, nobody could be sure of it but myself, though the three flags were left as some kind of token. Once down in Horton-in-Ribblesdale, I downed two speedy pints of mild and bitter in the pub – the first beer I had ever really enjoyed – and took the long road home. The run had taken me twelve hours, and I arrived back to play in an orchestral concert in the evening. Walton's 'Crown Imperial' will always recall for me the agonizing attacks of cramp which beset me throughout the performance. The new piece, 'Orb and Sceptre', had been a closely guarded secret, and we played the music from the previous coronation.

It was the longest and probably the most Quixotic run I ever took, though I once carried my oboe to the summit of The Calf as I thought it was an instrument that would sound well on a mountain top. A Loeillet sonata lost on the winds and a handful of Swaledale ewes. If I were called upon to single out the aspect of my secondary education which has left the most lasting stamp on my life, it would have to be the music, and to music I return. To say that I played under Barbirolli could be misleading, though that rarely prevents me from dropping it casually into conversation. To explain, Sir John had been asked to talk to the school on (his own title) 'The Conductor's Job'. He replied that he didn't think he was much good at talking – in the event it proved that he did himself less than justice – but would be pleased to take the school orchestra through a rehearsal.

Two movements of Haydn's London Symphony formed the *chef d'oeuvre* of the forthcoming speech day concert, but we rehearsed for this rehearsal with more verve and apprehension than for any concert. I was fifteen years old and a very nervous second oboe, often to my secret shame relegated to second trumpet parts. From the spare, hunched figure on the rostrum, crouched over his baton with the eye of a Robespierre, the mesmeric influence of our guest conductor was sheer magic. As he explained concisely what he wanted, caught your eye electrically as he brought you in, frequently stopping to take the instrument from the leading 'cellist to demonstrate with clarity, here a cadence, there a crescendo, we were truly inspired and aware that this was an occasion when the whole amounted to far more than the sum of its constituent parts.

The House Music Competitions took place at the end of the Easter term, the finals constituting a concert on the last night, with an adjudicator of standing in the musical world. Chief by far of the influences which shaped my life were those of Michael Thornely, my House Tutor, later to succeed Bruce Lockhart as Headmaster of Sedbergh. Driving points home with the stem of a forensic and acrid-flavoured pipe, his ready grin tending to the wolfish, he managed the House with an urbane, Mikadoesque humour. It was Michael who, mostly outside school hours, put the muscles and sinews on my skeletal tastes in music and literature, and steered my discernment between the lasting and the trivial. We wrote two small operettas together of which I am still quite proud, and he taught me most of what I know about singing. He also schooled the House Orchestra.

The competitions, as jealously waged by staff as by boys, were held in three sections. The first was a pair of songs in unison, known traditionally as the House Shout. Anyone with broken voice who was not demonstrably tone-deaf was dragooned into the team. The main song chosen was usually a Beethoven or Schubert, especially if it was suspected that the adjudicator did not speak German (which I had to learn purely phonetically), as this would, it was hoped, offset inaccuracies in diction. The contrasting song would be an Old English ballad of the Lane Wilson variety, extolling Phyllis or Chloë or some other pastoral pin-up, native wood notes coming strangely from the strapping band of Spartan warriors and front row forwards uncomfortably gathered to praise her.

The instrumental section was allowed twelve minutes' playing time. Our chief rivals were Powell House, who seemed to attract the musical élite, and at that time boasted the Gwilt brothers and a handful of other members of the National Youth Orchestra. They put in impeccable solo performances and chamber groups. Our strength lay in the ensembles. Michael would recruit as large an orchestra as School House could muster, around thirty strong, and chose pieces with a sturdy rhythmic appeal – Handel, Vivaldi and such – which were fun to play. His methods of achieving the desired results were characteristically unorthodox. I remember winning one year with the 'Praeludium' by Jarnefelt, an irresistibly jolly piece with a delicious oboe part and a wistful slow passage with solo violin, which our coach christened 'The Cow', as our interpretation put him in mind of a dying one.

Little touches of stage management were as carefully rehearsed as the notes. Here we would knowingly grin round at each other (an oboist in action can only do it with his eyebrows) as if at some shared joke, and there the double bass – who had his part unobtrusively marked in chalk on his instrument – would pretend to exchange a quip with the cymbal player, to be silently rebuked by Dave, who was conducting. This sort of thing would infuriate competing purists in the audience, but went down well with judges, who could see we were so obviously enjoying making music. Our sheer size was another bone of contention. We would, deliberately provocative, space out our procession on to the stage, and we must have looked like the entrance of the royal children in *The King and I.*

The third section of the competition was the unaccompanied House Quartet, in which Dave and I sang bass and tenor for four consecutive years and won the shield for the last three. Treble and alto changed of necessity as young voices broke. Once Sir Stuart Wilson made us proud honorary members of his Society for the Prevention of Cruelty to Dotted Notes. Bruce Lockhart coached us in the quartet, and practices were held in unaccustomed domestic comfort in their lovely drawing-room, the wide bay of mullioned windows looking far out over the fells. Mrs B.L. would sit knitting by the fire, offering the occasional quiet advice and comment from the sofa. The music of Quilter, the poems of Herrick and, above both, the scent of hyacinths which at that time of the year pervaded the room, bring it all back to me in detail. The music finals over, the school descended to the chapel for a late end-of-term service, after which we finished off packing for next morning's departure for the different world of the holidays.

7

Home for
the Holidays

Prawning beyond the light

An INEVITABLE, NOT UNHEALTHY, RESULT OF BOARDING SCHOOL education is that home takes on a status of unalloyed Utopia. The end of term, culminating for us in a long, euphoric train journey to Euston, saw a gathering of returning exiles on a frenetic high, induced by nothing more toxic than the prospect of a few weeks of unorganized freedom, unwonted comfort and home cooking. Reaction to school uniform brought out a rash of lurid kipper ties and bright brown shoes with crêpe soles of a thickness liable to give the wearer an attack of vertigo. This jazzy ensemble was worn for the journey only – even the informality of home demanded rather more sober attire.

The return fare was covered, unbelievably, by a five-pound note. It was crisp, white and impressively big, endorsed romantically with the signatures of previous owners, to which I added my own, like a pyramid letter. Somehow that was supposed to counter the counterfeit. With a fiver you really felt you had some money, and kept it carefully in a wallet, not crumpled in a trouser pocket. School trunks were sent PLA – not Port of London Authority, but Passenger Luggage in Advance. This ensured they would be delivered at home in time for packing to go back again. The advance bit was a polite fiction.

A splendidly acoustic feature of the journey was a travelling orchestra. We would start in the early stages with quite a respectable ensemble and could tackle anything from Humperdinck to 'My Home in Passadena', but we would lose a couple of fiddles at Crewe and a French horn at Rugby and by the time we approached London the group had dwindled to a very oddly assorted quintet. As the train slowed down for a station, the programme would switch to a round – 'London's Burning' or 'Frère Jacques' or 'Three Blind Mice'. The shock of successive strings, brass and woodwind proclaiming 'Fire! Fire!' has a deterrent effect, even when the compartment seems half empty, far more persuasive than the official 'reserved' signs stuck flimsily on the windows.

There used to be one of those lengthy, inconsequential shaggy dog stories about a man who was employed to conduct elephants from Victoria to Euston. Sensibly, he walked with his charges. We used to manage the trip in reverse with elephantine suitcases, Patrick and a 'cello and took the Underground. I loved London in those days. There was no Victoria Line, and the excursion involved a change of trains and levels at Charing Cross. The impatient sportsmen who habitually run up the escalators would find their passage bulkily hampered by Patrick and 'cello, rising majestically out of the depths, staring fixedly and unheedingly ahead, a returning Orpheus with a particularly cumbersome lute. Repeated hints that the piccolo was a delightful instrument and had he thought about a change fell on deaf ears. Secretly I am sure we would have missed the eccentric Bertha anyway.

We had moved to Eastbourne in 1950. A seaside town is never entirely urban, and Eastbourne gave far more imminent access to unspoilt countryside than most, but the change from our agrarian seclusion in Hertfordshire was integral. In contrast to a sleepy village, where wartime Ministry of Information films had been now and again projected in the back of a visiting army lorry, we were now surrounded by seven cinemas and four theatres. We did not find this unwelcome. After all, we knew the town – it bristled with Mum's relations – and an unvaried diet of rustic charm would undoubtedly have staled eventually, and might even have turned our love of the countryside to bored dislike.

Eastbourne was recovering from its wartime injuries, licking wounds which were slow to heal. We hardly saw the battle scars – as a nation we were so used to them – but after a scant five years, though débris had been largely cleared, the work of rebuilding had scarcely begun. Wrecks were still visible in the Channel at low tide, old mines were constantly being washed up on the beach, and unexploded shells were a hazard on the Downs where we went butterflying. Fences and hoardings hid unsightly gaps where hotels and shops had vanished. No. 20, The Avenue, home to a warren of children, my mother among them, a generation before us, had completely disappeared, leaving a wilderness of willow herb and wild buddleia where moths and butterflies abounded. The battered tower of the Town Hall topped a likely looking film set for Mons or Arras, and our neighbouring St Anne's Church was a gutted, haunted shell.

We had no television. Few had. Some family friends had a set, as big as a respectable sideboard with a screen the size of a shaving mirror, but reception was wildly erratic, beset with recurring snowstorms, and it was no substitute for the cinema. There were no transistors. A portable wireless set was so called because it ran off a hugh dry battery and could be moved from room to room, but it was far too heavy to take for a long walk. The beaches were correspondingly quiet. Gramophone records were thick, brittle and weighty and lasted all of three minutes. A needle lasted for one record only, and you had to remember to keep the handle fully wound.

In 1950 the egg ration was one per person per week; butter was a generous three ounces. Mum mixed ours with a substantial buffer of margarine to make it go further, a trick which she continued until more than a decade later when I succeeded in convincing her that rationing had stopped and the price difference was negligible. How did we survive those hot summers without refrigerators? Meat safes either hung outside on a shady wall or were built-in and open to the exterior, shielded by metal gauze. Hair and scent sprays worked with a rubber bulb, and charcoal fixative had to be blown on to canvas with a bent tube, leaving one breathless and red of face. Fresh air sprays had not appeared; for comfort we burnt joss sticks in the loo until Airwick came to the rescue of the fastidious. Trousers needed regular creasing and socks wouldn't stay up without garters.

Socks, indeed, hung nightly outside from every window sill in the home, along with towels and bathing trunks. There were no washing machines apart from Mum and our indispensible 'Aunt' West, who spent half her life up to the elbows in suds. Did we not wash as much in those days? Baths were an adventure rather than a relaxation. Hot water was dispensed fitfully by a bad-tempered geyser which administered either frost-bite or third degree burns but little in between. Twice it exploded out of sheer malevolence and had to be bracketed back on to the wall.

Hanging out washing was problematical, for should a clothes line be in view, a lynx-eyed vigilante regiment of elderly, retired ladies would gripe indignantly to police and press. An old dear in the top flat summoned an embarrassed young constable, complaining that a man over the way refused to draw his curtains when he stripped at night. She said she could see him clearly from her bathroom. The policeman confessed he could see nothing. 'No! But just you stand here on the lavatory seat. There! He's at it again!'

The formidable ladies of Eastbourne had homed on the resort from a thousand verandahs in far-flung Somerset Maugham outposts. Caveat vendor! When fashionable shops required to change the costumes displayed on their window dummies, each lifeless Galatea had to be draped in a shapeless canvas tube. Should a plaster limb or moulded breast be ever so momentarily exposed coyly to the view, the ensuing outrage would speedily demonstrate why Hitler never stood a chance. Less robust emporia would simply pull down the blinds and shut up shop till the metamorphosis was complete.

We three felt a whiff of the matriarchal grapeshot. Early on summer mornings we would climb into our bathing trunks and on to our bikes and race down to the sea for a dip, never dreaming that our naked torsos could bring the blush of shame to the cheek of authority. Complaints rumbled. Thereafter we sped down encumbered by dressing-gowns which streamed out behind us. Our own great-aunts, three resident in Eastbourne, were all rooted in the British Raj, but in their three different ways, one through seasoned wisdom, one through a hazily benign tolerance and the other through the rollicking bats in her belfry, they would have dismissed such pettiness out of hand.

Great Aunt Ella was the senior of the trio, just sixty years older than I, tall, slim and imperious. She would walk, proudly erect, down to the shops with a shapeless basket, an ancient, wide-brimmed gardening straw shading her head, her drab ensemble entirely eclipsed by an unconscious air of regal authority. Aunt Ella radiated ramrod self-discipline, though I once caught her relaxing with a cigarette, held delicately with a wire hairpin lest she stain her fingers. Instinctively I never told anyone about this.

Old canvases from days in India – landscapes, flowers, birds and native characters – lay in odd corners in her house and testified to a far from meagre talent long set aside. Her love and artistry in the twilight of her years found sole expression in the rare blooms and controlled abundance of her beautiful garden, beloved of moths in the scented evening, when she would often summon me if anything exciting appeared. Clematis rampaged over the mellow Victorian red brick walls and roof, so chosen that at least one variety would be in bloom from early spring until well into November.

Great-nephews were, it went without saying, an available work-force. We were never given pocket money on a regular basis, but when pockets were light we could always earn it. 'When I was a girl,' she would say sternly (she pronounced it 'gairl' in the Victorian manner), 'the going rate was one shilling. In view of the rising cost of living this should now be five shillings. However, with regard to the decadence of modern youth I shall give you half-a-crown.' It was pretty good really, as it represented ten threepenny ice creams, or three visits to the cinema if you went in at the front and worked your way back in the dark.

We turned our hands to most things. We became adepts at interior decorating. Paints were less easy of application then, before the days of plastic emulsions. Distemper had less covering power and tended to show every brush stroke. Oil-based paint was sticky and intractable. Doors, cupboards and wainscots had to be painted dark underneath, covered with a lighter coat and then grained and stippled with combs and balding old brushes to represent oak, which I'm sure they were underneath anyway.

Great Aunt Ethel, tall and massive, was a study in opposites. All the Aunts had had their large houses converted into flats and lived off the income in the garden basements. Aunt Ethel's big flat was more than untidy. It had a permanent air of a huge family either just moving in or just moving out. Nothing, in the course of a long life, had ever been thrown away, and most of it lay on every chair, couch and table and in heaps in corners. She was notoriously unpunctual. Not to the minute or hour, but often a day or so. She loved parties, but invariably one of us would be dispatched to get her. Tim would introduce her: 'This is my great-aunt, the late Mrs Woodhouse.' She would chuckle delightedly.

Great Aunt Ethel came back to England with other members of the family in 1944, cheerfully unable to cope with a life without servants and sunshine. She had never had to pick up anything she dropped, so why start now? Eastbourne usually got a share of any sunshine that was going – it still does – but she had a huge greenhouse built adjoining the house as a 'sun parlour' and, like Milne's sailor, regularly sat in the punitive heat and basked until she was saved.

Not that her life was an idle one. Aunt Ethel taught English language and literature to successive classes of Siamese students who adored her. The flat was hung with erudite notices with a literary flavour. By the front door bell-push was a placard with the legend, 'Though we seem dead, we do but sleep.' To which we added a school report, 'Will only work satisfactorily under constant pressure.' Curiously in the hallway hung a builder's diagram of the plumbing system. Tim emended this like a medieval map with drawings of dolphins and galleons and sea serpents and remarks such as 'Here be dragons'.

She was a compulsive devotee of sales rooms, a fatal flaw in one so given to talk and gesticulation. One day she turned up with a pair of enormous steel banjos, which she had acquired along with a chamber-pot or two and a fire-screen. 'I thought the boys might like these. I didn't realize I'd bought them.' At Christmas she would meticulously cut up last year's cards with pinking shears and post them to all her friends. We were quite likely to get the one we sent her the year before, neatly serrated with a bit of pink ribbon through it.

She had a thirst for anything academic and was especially interested in the more scientific side of our pursuit of butterflies and moths, asking searching questions and requiring detailed precision in the answers. This of course caused me to think and clarify my own ideas. Her quest for the precise (the incisiveness of her mind was a marked contrast to the chaos of her surroundings) often led her on to dangerous ground. I remember overhearing a conversation with my father when I was about twelve years old:

'Sam, what exactly is the translation of the *anus*?'

'The arsehole, Auntie,' replied Dad bluntly.

'Really! Sam!'

'I'm truly sorry, but there really is no other word in English that will exactly fit. "Bottom" is too broad a term. Better stick to the Latin!'

The last of the three elderly Graces, Great Aunt Edith, lived in a spacious, late Georgian style house in Burlington Place near the sea front. She had filled the rooms from cellar to attic with shabby second-hand furniture and let them out as theatrical digs. The house was known to the lesser lights of the profession as 'Ma Maloney's'. As tall as her sisters, she had been by common consent the beauty of the family, wilful and headstrong, and in her old age was still strikingly handsome. And wilful.

I remember this great-aunt when I was small as by far the best story-teller of a bunch all highly gifted at the game. Her voice was hypnotic, musically articulate with fastidious diction. Whenever I hear the tones of the late Dame Sybil Thorndike, the likeness to Aunt Edith brings me up with a jolt. She had a luxuriant imagination and a fine ear for drama. In her seventies she had turned to melodrama. On occasion lucid, mischievous and cuttingly amusing, she lived for the most part in a confused morass of indecision. She would pose on the landing – careful that the light from the big square window gave just the right setting – fling a forearm across her brow like Irving, and declaim, 'My God! – I can't think!'

When time hung heavy she would decide to move all her furniture. This of course necessitated a task force, and she would telephone early in the morning for 'The Boys'. It usually happened on fine days when we wished anything but to be pent indoors. The most notable of these reshuffles involved the contents of the entire house and we were unable to escape. Staying with us at the time were our Tippetts cousins, Maisie's two elder boys, Edward, who was my age, and David, a young monkey who partnered Patrick in an unpredictable, rascally duo. Even Patrick and David, acknowledged experts, were unable to extract pocket money from Aunt Edith, who blandly ignored the convention of a day's pay for a day's work. We never got even a glass of squash. In glum dismay we found that we had to shift settees, armchairs and dressing tables from room to room, from floor to floor, under the capricious direction of Aunt Edith, interspersed with countless encores of the 'Can't think' tableau. This was varied at intervals with both fists pressed against the temples and 'This is getting beyond me! I must go down for my medicine!'

Tim was trying to keep notes of the manoeuvres as we gasped under the weight of solid mahogany bedsteads and squeezed wardrobes through doors scarcely wide enough to take them. By the late afternoon he reckoned we had moved practically everything back into the locations they had occupied when we started in the morning. He and Edward decided to investigate the medicine. From a sideboard in the basement they extracted a squat, green bottle. 'I thought so,' said Edward, uncorking and sniffing it. 'Neat Scotch!' We liberated a quart bottle of India Pale Ale which had been hiding behind it in the dark recess, and made hurriedly for the beach.

Edward combined a precocious taste for beer with ambitions directed at county Rugby and a career in the Army. A delightful, grave companion who thought deeply and spoke sparingly, he was also an asthmatic, but managed later to conceal this somehow and get himself passed fit for National Service. Tragically, on an exercise in Germany, Edward and his companions were shut up in a hay barn for a temporary night's lodging. Some unhinged idiot, for a joke, fired a Very pistol into the straw. Most escaped, but the asphyxiating smoke must have been too much for Edward, for he perished in the fire.

Always active, we explored most of East Sussex on our bicycles with the butterfly nets. Tim and Patrick had estimable machines, Raleighs, with drop handlebars and three-speed gears. I acquired a high, sturdy, sit-up-and-beg bone shaker for thirty bob from an Australia-bound emigrant greengrocer who had bought it second-hand in the 1930s. To make the challenge exciting, we would often rule a straight line on the map and stick to it rigorously, cycling over Down and heathland, fording streams till we arrived at the chosen destination. There was relatively little traffic on the roads. With luck we could freewheel, without pedalling once, down the road from the top of Beachy Head, into the town past Holywell, along the length of the sea front and fetch up at the Burlington Hotel almost opposite the pier, where a slight rise brought us finally to a halt.

The pier was a ready source of diversion, the nearest thing prim Eastbourne had to the cheerful fairground vulgarity of Brighton or Southend. Tim was fascinated by its lattice of angled piles and girders and would sketch it by the hour. At the summit of the pavilion was (I dare say still is) the original 'Camera Obscura', where a rotating lens above projected the living panorama of the sea front down on to a sort of clay dew-pond around which you sat, a Victorian marvel of science. Scant pocket money fed our gambling instincts. Halfpennies were slotted into machines where a ball bearing was spun round vertically and with luck landed in one of a series of cups, whereupon you got your money back and were given another try. It was Tim who discovered accidentally that if you put two consecutive halfpennies in before activating the trigger, the ball came back whether you won or lost. We consequently spent whole wet mornings on the machines and struggled home with pockets heavily weighed down with piles of copper.

Huge prizes, dolls and ornaments, were never won but stood permanently at the back of the stalls to tempt the punter. I made one phenomenal score at the rifle range and settled on a hideous pot monkey, leering nastily with a crack running across his tummy. 'You can't 'ave 'im, 'e's broke!' declared the girl. 'I know the feeling well. I insist on having him!' I said, and duly took the gargoyle home. The rifle sights were all slightly askew. Patrick came to recognize each weapon so well, aiming off accordingly, that he was clearly liable to lose them money. So they compromised by employing him on the stall. His stallholding showed such flair that eventually he ran a postcard booth near the Wish Tower, where two nuns would visit him every morning and chortle over the risqué offerings of Donald McGill.

One little booth housed the clairvoyant, a surprisingly unremarkable, dumpy little lady, partial to bottles of milk stout. We never had our fortunes told – the silver-crossed palm bit seemed an unwarrantable expense for information that time would make apparent in due course anyway – but she inspired a drawing from Tim. An irate customer had just bopped her on the head with a mallet, scattering playing cards, crystal ball and stout bottles. The caption was 'Striking the Happy Medium'. It kept us and Tim, then around fifteen, in fits of helpless laughter for weeks. He was always delighted with his own jokes.

Next door a man cut lightning silhouettes. Tim had, even in those early days, the enviable ability to capture a likeness in about thirty seconds with a few swift pencil strokes. He thought he could be on to a good thing. So he duly set himself up on the promenade with easel and sketchboard, with Patrick as barker and a few friends (I was away somewhere with the net), and a placard announcing 'Timothy will draw your portrait for one shilling'.

Business was brisk. A large crowd gathered to watch, the promenade became impassable and, inevitably, a solid guardian of the law loomed heavily to sort out the congestion. Had he a licence? Tim was unaware that he needed one. Tim and his assistants were escorted, with their trappings, to the police station. By one of those fortuitous coincidences, the Chief Constable, who happened to be there – I cannot think they would have been hauled in front of him in the normal line of his duty – was an Old Sedberghian. The illustrious officer blandly demanded his own portrait. For free. The result must have pleased him, for Tim was packed off with a caution, having promised, rather crossly, not to unsettle the peaceful resort again. He didn't get his easel back for a week.

An advantage to youngsters growing up in a seaside resort is the abundance of ice-cream parlours. In those days ice-cream was largely made on the various premises, not retailed in prepacked foil. We became connoisseurs of such shops and stalls. We would discuss their relative merits and quality as in later years we would come to deride or extol the beers of different breweries, again more diverse than they are today. Our unrivalled favourites were the Notarriani Brothers, whom we called 'The Sloppers', for they disdained those meticulous ladles which meted out a uniform hemisphere atop the mouth of a cone, but scraped their ice-cream in liberally from huge wooden spoons. A sixpenny cornet was a meal in itself, full to the nethermost tip. No disappointment in life is more truly desiccated than the empty wafer tip of an inefficiently filled ice-cream cone.

Out of season the sea, the beaches and the chalk cliffs were quieter and more our own. The rough flats beyond Langney Point and the shoreline of Pevensey Bay were havens for migrant wading birds late in the year and again in early spring, and many spent the winter there in large flocks. I miss the proximity of the sea, for it adds an extra dimension to life, its mood ever changing and its prospect ever shifting, a constant and uncompromising reminder that there are aspects of nature that man can never tame or subdue. In the height of the holiday season we would get out early to avoid the crowds, when the shore was still clean from the night tide and untenanted save for an old cormorant who perched dejectedly every morning on a tall pole at the end of a breakwater with his wings hung out to dry, until the shouts of the first early bathers would send him flapping mournfully off in weary dudgeon.

We lived on sandwiches then, hair permanently sticky from the sea water, bodies tanned mahogany and covered dustily from morning splash to evening tub in a patina of dried salt and chalk. We bathed from the rocks near the lighthouse, far below the famous Beachy Head leap in a cove seemingly inaccessible, but approached down a hidden smugglers' path where the holiday-makers never ventured. Many a time before leaving the cliff-top for this narrow descent, on turf soon to be covered in picnicking crowds, I have watched fox cubs romping round the resting vixen in the dawn, or a peregrine swooping on a rabbit, and wondered what the thoughts of the crowds would be if they knew what dramas were enacted in the spot so shortly before their arrival.

As a rule the only people we saw on the shore were solitary prawn fishermen, loaded with nets, crunching their heavy, nailed boots westwards at the foot of the chalk cliffs. Inevitably this was a sport we had to try, and it was only a matter of time before we took up prawn fishing in earnest. From early childhood I had been fascinated by whiskery crustaceans. Before the war, in Filey in Yorkshire, we had daily watched crabs being boiled and dressed in a cobbled yard, tipped into the cauldron a dull brown and emerging steaming, pink and red and smelling delicious. In Morecambe, on the opposite coast, we had seen the old fishwives, dressed in black with white caps and aprons, shelling the shrimps with their teeth with astonishing speed. Shortly after the war, the Ministry of Food, or Health, or perhaps Ag and Fish, declared with squeamish shudders that the method was unhygienic – it probably was – and a centuries-old skill was discontinued. Shrimp shelling sans teeth is a fussy business, so the task took immeasurably longer and up went the price of potted shrimps.

Prawning 'beyond the Light', notwithstanding the high price of prawns, would not earn a man a living today – if it ever did – and I stress this lest any entrepreneur should be tempted to try it as a commercial venture. Also I can see the apprehensive faces of old friends reading this, fearful that I might encourage would-be rivals. Prawn fishermen are furtive, secret souls who jealously guard the locations of their favourite pools. 'Nobby's 'Ole' and 'Sid's Gully' will not be found on the map, but mention them to one of the initiates as he gets his nose into his third pint – especially if you have purchased it for him – and he might tell you a tale or two. Norse sagas are more widely known and considerably bloodier, but the exploits of such prawners as Fred the Tax have a haunting, riveting enchantment to rival those of Eric the Red, Wulf the Unsightly or any of them.

In the early days our tackle was borrowed from friends, a pair of prawning twins who have since both become Bishops and fishers of men. Basically one needs a set of half a dozen 'gin nets' and a long pole with a hook. A gin consists of a shallow net slung from a fifteen-inch circular hoop, surmounted by a half-hoop standing vertically, at the apex of which is attached four or five feet of strong line threaded with cork floats. We would scavenge the dustbins behind fishmongers for plaice frames, the flat carcase discarded when the fish had been filleted. These, the gamier the better, were skewered into the base of each net as bait. After tramping the rocks fragrantly for an hour or so, we reached the prawning grounds a couple of hours before low tide. The retreating tide revealed holes and channels in the chalk into which the nets were lowered gently with the hook. Pulling up the nets in rotation and replacing them further out, the transparent, clicking prawns were scooped up into a bag slung round the neck. After slack water the sport continued for an hour, now moving backwards on the slippery rocks, studded treacherously with limpets which can rasp raw a careless hand or knee. It was imperative to leave off in time and get round the point before the accelerating tide caught us. Any later the only escape would have been an impossible perpendicular climb among the raucous, mocking laughter of the nesting gulls.

Somehow prawns never roused our sympathy as we tipped our catches into a pan of bubbling brine. This was hunting for the pot, which has a separate, though stringent, set of morals. We also caught the occasional lobster – we always took a length of string to disarm him, just in case – and the flattened velvet swimming crabs, ultramarine in life and arising a bright vermilion from the pan.

By way of contrast, we arrived home for one holiday to be told there was a marauding mouse nightly roaming the kitchen. We had no trap. 'Don't worry! I'll catch him!' Patrick was confidently reassuring. That evening Tim and I laughed prodigiously at his preparations. He tied a length of string round a lump of toasted cheese, the other end secured to a pencil. Over the cheese, on the floor, he used the pencil to prop up an inverted biscuit tin at an angle.

In the morning, despite our ribbing, the structure had collapsed.

How to find out if the mouse was there? I suggested the old mothing trick, where a postcard is slid under an imprisoning tumbler against the wall. A broad sheet of card was inserted in the same manner and the tin turned over. There was our adventurer, bravely leaping up the sides but slipping vainly on the smooth metal. Patrick's trap was a demonstrable success, but what now? 'Send for a cat?' I suggested tentatively. 'Cotton wool and ether!' offered Tim. Patrick was incensed. It was his mouse, by right of capture, and he felt responsible. 'I'll let it go in the garden.' Perhaps he was thinking of catching it again the next night. We eventually succeeded in convincing him that if the culprit were released anywhere less than a mile away, it would unerringly find its way back to our kitchen. Patrick duly set off on his bike with the mouse aboard and gave it its freedom in the ornamental gardens at Hamden Park.

Denied mice, Patrick kept tortoises in the garden. He still does, along with spacious outdoor aviaries full of exotic birds. In Eastbourne you don't have to bed tortoises down in boxes for the winter, as there is so rarely any penetrating frost. They burrow into the garden and reappear in the spring. Our original huge tortoise nearly forty years ago was called Max for short. Max was short for Quintus Fabius Maximus Cunctator, the delaying general who eventually clobbered Hannibal. Max in due course of time laid an egg and had to be rechristened, Quinta Fabia Maxima Cunctatrix. She was still known as Max for short. The egg, despite weeks of incubation in the airing cupboard, never hatched. We found this was not a new problem when we heard on the wireless a naturalist from Baltimore talking about one of the larger tortoises on one of the smaller Galapagos Islands. The accent and the doleful account inspired one of our poems:

> On distant isle Galapagate
> There lives alone a wistful turdle.
> He'd dearly love to prapagate.
> The giant, sadly, just ain't furdle.

Gilbert White had a way with tortoises and, taken out of context, an entry in his diary for 1 July 1780 had a special poignancy for us:

> We put Timothy into a tub of water, & found that he sunk gradually & walked on the bottom of the tub: he seemed quite out of his element, & was much dismayed. This species seems not at all amphibious.

8

Of Savoyards,
South Bank and Strings

Garden Tiger moth

THE HIGHLIGHTS OF THE HOLIDAYS WERE ALWAYS ACHIEVED when the Birdsalls were united with the Scotts from Knowle House, either in Eastbourne or at their home in Surrey. Poor days there must have been, but in retrospect life seems to have been compounded of snow at Christmas and long, hot summers of sunshine and laughter. So much laughter. Jennifer and I were of the same age, as were Charles and Tim, then Sally and Patrick. Dave was often with us, down from Carlisle, and Sally's close friend Jackie spent most of her holidays with the Scotts. Jackie was really part of the family. It was the sort of scenario beloved of Enid Blyton, whose books of the Famous Five we used to read irreverently aloud in turns amid convulsive laughter, for we assisted the narrative with our own lists of random nouns and adjectives; taken in rotation, they were inserted whenever the reader paused for one. There was even a dog, Chike, short for Tchaikowski, which he couldn't spell.

Knowle House was in Betjeman Country. The colourful garden ran down to a wooded golf course which extended to the old Bishop's Palace at Addington. The village and its little flint church, where we regularly attended church parades of a Sunday, singing the hymns lustily in parts to compete with the penetrating contralto of the postmistress, seemed a world away from nearby Croydon and the busy Metropolis. The gracious house, white walled and green pantiled, sparkled indoors and smelt of lavender furniture polish.

Charles, to my secret unease, was often treated as something of a butt, though with his perpetual good humour he took it all with a grin. Extravagantly pompous remarks would be attributed to him which he would never have dreamt of saying. 'Do not the daffodils make a brave display? – as Charles was about to say!' Often known as Bernsteen, after Charlie of the Runyon stories which we loved, he really shared the engaging simplicity of those gullible – and essentially honest – rogues of the Bronx. A naturally gifted games player, he also had a mechanical bent and was never happier as a youngster than when garaging the car for his father or revving it round and round the circular drive in front of the house.

Sally, the youngest, was in looks, expression and personality astonishingly like Tim, whom as a little girl she patently adored. Inseparable, both had the same colouring, the same scowl at times and the same capacity to smoulder. If Tim was 'in one of his moods', you could safely bet that Sally would be in one of hers, and the devil of a job it was to jolly them out of it. On the other hand, when the sun broke through it was dazzling, and both were likely to choke uncontrollably with infectious merriment. Sally showed early talent as an artist and has developed her gifts professionally since childhood.

Though tall and fair, sweet and lively, and wont to sigh in sympathy for little, unadopted roads, Jennifer was no Betjeman girl. She had too much sense of humour. We did play tennis – once even as partners in a tournament – but I was even less proficient on the court than I was on the cricket field. I wore long white flannels for tennis in those days; shorts were considered a bit showy and smacked of 'side' unless you were really good. Charles and their cousin, Susan, upheld our honour and made the semi-finals. After-wards, as we were rewarded with lemon barley and Jennifer asked for – and got – sherry, to our indignant envy, she congratulated the pair.

'Susan rose to the occasion. Like a prawn . . . to – what would a prawn rise to?'

'Seaweed?' I suggested. Rotten plaice frames would have spoilt the eulogy.

'Do they really?'

'Oh, certainly,' I lied.

'Rose like a prawn to a piece of seaweed.'

We doted on prawns. You couldn't get frozen Norwegian sacks of them in the early fifties and 'scampi' we would have assumed to be a musical annotation. Homespun Valentine cards depicted them, and we used to send each other encouraging slogans. 'Mrs Whitaker of Woking Feeds her Family on Prawns.' Floreat crustacea.

The girls boarded at what seemed to us an untypically forward-looking school for young ladies in London's Queen's Gate. They wore no uniform but they all looked very pretty and intimidating to a shy young man as they clustered and chattered on a balcony high above the pavement like departing swallows. It was from this perch that the impulsive Sally, unable to resist the target of a bald head below, dropped a blancmange or some other glutinous concoction with more accuracy than acumen on a Minor Ambassador. We all thought it might start a war, like Jenkins and his ear, but ruffled diplomatic relations were presumably smoothed.

These, then, were the founder members of the ASDPH, the Association of Semi-Demented Poetry Hailers, who sang Sullivan's 'Hail, Poetry!', unaccompanied, in parts, at the drop of a hat, on station platforms, on disused lighthouses, in bursting telephone boxes and, especially, during communal chores such as washing-up.

We had our differences. Jennifer, Dave and I preferred Ovaltine last thing, while the others swore fiercely by Horlicks, and the Battle of the Bedtime Beverages was waged with mock acrimony every evening. But we all shared a passionate love of the operas of Gilbert and Sullivan.

In my teens admittedly I placed Gilbert and Sullivan on too high a pedestal. In later years they found their rightful drawer in my music cabinet, between the lighter classical operas and the best of musical comedy, but I found, as so many others must have done, that the music of Sullivan was my gateway to appreciating classical music. We followed the D'Oyly Carte Company with devotion from Streatham Hill to Golders Green, with Sadlers Wells, the Savoy and Prince's theatres in between, mostly in the gods, though once or twice in a season we were taken in style. On our own, modest visits we would start to queue around morning coffee time, under colourful golf umbrellas when it rained, singing all the choruses and disappearing in staggered groups for alfresco lunches at barrows and stalls. Where conventional people would take a box of chocolates to the theatre, I preferred a bag of whelks. If you joined the queue early you could claim one of the little wooden, folding queuing seats specially provided by the company on the pavement outside. It is a fact of history that Richard D'Oyly Carte first instigated the theatre queue. Before this, theatre doors were flung open to a wild free-for-all, patrons scrambling dangerously over rows of seats to reach the front of the upper circle. It was glorious to watch our idols from the stalls, but the informality of our days spent waiting for cheap seats – two or three shillings in those days – made us feel almost part of the show and were indisputably more fun. We even developed a nodding acquaintance with some of the stars.

The first years of the Fifties were great ones for the D'Oyly Carte, dominated by giants such as Martyn Green and Darrell Fancourt, the former figuratively only as he was tiny, dapper and mercurial, the latter a giant in stature as well, and in performance often terrifying. Nobody has ever echoed Fancourt's grisly Mikado laugh. Ella Halman played the contralto roles, Gilbert's old maids, and as Lady Jane, in *Patience*, played the 'cello herself on stage with resolute application, a feat which, to my knowledge, no other exponent has emulated. The girls swooned over Leonard Osborn, the principal tenor, red-haired, loose-limbed, impossibly handsome and a magnificent dancer. There was a beguiling story, current at the time but not involving us, of two girls begging the stage doorman to let them see their hero as he had such lovely white teeth. The doorman returned with the message that Mr Osborn was at present in the bath, but if they were to wait a few minutes he would send his teeth down to them.

An acid test for visitors was their opinion, elicited and reported on by one or other of us, of Gilbert and Sullivan, especially the ability and willingness to join us round the piano. Jennifer was more than competent to play for us, so we never needed adult accompaniment. There were other criteria by which we judged our elders, but this was the most stringent. A peak of our amateur operatic career was Michael Thornely's production of *The Pirates of Penzance* at Sedbergh, in which we were well represented, with Dave as a courteous Blimp of a Major General and Tim as a burring, West Country Samuel, while I played the tenor lead. *The Westmorland Gazette* wrote: 'J.A. Birdsall in the role of Frederic, the Pirate Apprentice, was outstanding. His incisive approach to the part, his freedom of movement, and keen sense of timing and climax contributed to a noteworthy interpretation.' Whether the pun was intentional, I know not. I don't get reviews like that any more. Westmorland has been bureaucratically buried for many years, but *The Westmorland Gazette* lives on. With such a tradition for palpable discernment, so it should.

My 'leading lady' at the time, with a powerful, very near coloratura treble voice, is now Vice Admiral Sir Jock Slater, KCB, LVO, and Chief of Fleet Support, a Gilbertian turn up if ever there was one. I am told on good authority that a member of his crew during the Falklands campaign had somehow obtained a photograph of the 'Mabel' of that bygone show, and it constituted the principal pin-up in the mess. In my own brief naval career, in the chorus of *HMS Pinafore* in 1950, the (acting, radical) First Lord of the Admiralty, Sir Joseph Porter, KCB, was played with agile pomposity by Giles (now Sir Giles) Shaw. He might make it for real yet. Another MP, Bob Rhodes-James, was, even earlier, a strong-voiced, winsome Elsie Maynard in *The Yeomen of the Guard*. I would be interested to find out how many (and which) of our representative guardians at Westminster have played principal parts in Gilbert and Sullivan opera. And which parts. It is tempting to suggest a few possibilities, but it could get my publishers into trouble. One young friend of mine, a hilariously shady Duke of Plazatoro (Ltd) in his salad days, has become the youngest ever director of Courtaulds. A moral must lurk somewhere, but one which I am at pains not to draw.

The comment 'noteworthy', applied to me by the *Gazette*, was greeted by the rest with ribald approval. In our own private patois most things were 'worthy'. A sporty flat cap was known as a 'dogworthy'. Embarrassing situations were 'blushworthy'. A random kitten who was unable to drink its milk without shivering in frissons of excitement was promptly christened 'Ditherworthy'. The other, more widely shared, variation was the suffix '-ers'. Knowle House was of course always Knowlers, though this caused mild censure when the address was written as such on envelopes. The thing really started as a parody on our complicated traditional school slang, which we secretly found ridiculous and vaguely uncomfortable. As was our habit, we took refuge in extravagant exaggeration. A shout of 'Charles is scabbing tubbers!' meant that the miscreant was trying to get out of the washing-up, the regular chore of tub-drill. 'Golfers' was, naturally, the indispensible golf umbrella.

A further facet of our educational life, which we viewed first with discomfiture and later with contradictory affection, lay in the School Songs. To be fair, there were two rattling good ones, the only two as I remember to be regularly sung, one commemorating 'Winder' and the other 'The Long Run'; but others were demonstrably McGonagallworthy. For creaking phrase and doubtful rhyme, this claimed a special tenderness:

Come leave the Fives Court echoless,
    The Cricket Field deserted;
Today no House-run shall distress,
    No football boot be dirtied.
Come down from Winder's breezy height,
    Omit to burn the heather,
And sing this song with all your might,
    And take it up together.

Another, with a jingoistic flavour, has its place in our social history.

. . . the true Imperial tint
Is the dear, dull drab, the khaki-brown, of the Sedbergh OTC.

And there was the Cricket Song which exhorted us, 'Keep your temper and be jolly, And away with melancholy!' Stirring sentiments.

Hail to the name of the brave old game!
Wherever men are English and the flag's unfurled
You will find there Cricket and the willow and the wicket
And there's not a game to lick it in the whole wide world!

This last was guaranteed to infuriate the exiled clans, many of whom played useful straight bats in spite of their accidents of birth.

Inevitably our developing appetites for doggerel inspired much of our own. Most of it has passed, thankfully, into oblivion. Sitting one sunny day in the pergola, one of our frequent arguments, academic and not inimical, arose as to how it should be pronounced. The result was enshrined in verse and illustrated by Tim's quick pen.

> Matilda met a burglar
> Peering through the fuchsias.
> She kicked him in the purglar;
> He now needs several suchsias.

Our musical taste was widespread and by no means restricted to Sullivan. 'La Mer', which Tim and Sally used to sing in appalling English to tease me, knowing I loved it in French, 'Ain't She Sweet', 'I Wonder where my Baby is Tonight' – so many random tunes recall poignant memories. Mantovani's glissando strings in 'Charmaine' made a popular hit of the day, and we would play the record interminably, well into the small hours.

This was also an era of bubbling Hollywood song and dance extravaganzas, with Gene Kelly, Red Skelton, Fred Astaire, Anne Miller, Vera Ellen, Marge and Gower Champion, and the English side upheld in one production by an ageing, still debonair, Jack Buchanan. Our Uncle Farquhay was at the time producing a weekly show on television (one channel only in those days) called 'Current Release'. It was a forerunner of the sort of thing that Michael Parkinson and more recently Barry Norman have developed since; but it was, of course, live, and Farquhay confessed to occasional difficulty in keeping some of the interviewed stars sober for the cameras. He was sent tickets for all the trade previews which took place a day or so before the premières, but if he wanted a particular film for study or excerpts he would have it sent down to Lime Grove. So he used blandly to scrawl 'Complimentary – Admit 8' on a ticket of our choice, a ticket printed with all the lavishness of a ball invitation. We would troop in with notebooks and pencils trying to look mature and professional. Nobody, in fact, took any notice of us whatsoever.

Our favourite venue, the site of many of the sparkling escapist musicals, was the little MGM private theatre in Rose Crescent. Here one was ensconced in deep green leather armchairs, and at the appointed time a butler in full fig pulled a silken cord and opened the curtains to reveal the screen. Five minutes after the start the pros would all be fast asleep. We betrayed our callow youth by staying alert and enjoying every moment. Promptly, a minute or two before the end, the Press would come miraculously to life and everyone would file out without a word as though this was the most run-of-the-mill interlude in the world. It probably was for them. We would save our bursting comment and discussion until we were outside. On the first visit to this prestigious little cinema, Jennifer and I were by ourselves and had some difficulty in finding Rose Crescent. London was overrun by foreign visitors and we decided, after some vain attempts to be directed, to wait and ask the first obviously English person we met. Finally we saw a man in a dark suit with a rolled umbrella and black homberg hat. 'Gee, I'm sarry, kids,' he drawled in reply to our enquiry, 'I'm a stranger here myself.' Kids indeed! We were nearly seventeen.

A London teeming with foreigners is par for the course today and undeserving of comment, but that particular year, 1951, it was a novelty. This was the first influx of visitors since before the war, and for a special reason. For this was the summer of the Festival of Britain, the official end to post-war austerity, a Tonic to the Nation as it was officially described; and, as in the Great Exhibition of a century before, we were on show to the world.

Probably the most noticeable difference to today's visitor, if carried back to the London of my teens, would be the skyline. A mere six years after the Allied victory, stepping outside from Aldgate tube station, one saw St Paul's looming high, unobscured, across a broken, level waste. At ground level one was aware of a pervading shabbiness, but the skyline was a respite from the drab, punctuated by old unchallenged towers, domes and spires, most of them churches. Yet unborn were high-rise flats and office buildings, multi-storey car parks, urban motorways or the insolent Post Office Tower. For an eagle-eye view we used to pay sixpence and climb the three hundred and eleven worn spiral steps up Wren's Monument, counting all the way up and checking the tally all the way down again. There were no supermarkets and no shopping precincts, unless you count the Burlington Arcade. Covent Garden was much as Eliza Doolittle would have remembered it; Speakers' Corner was thronged with soap-box orators on the grass by Marble Arch; and Carnaby Street was just part of the route to my father's workplace at the Royal ENT Hospital in Golden Square, memorable to me only as the site of the house from which the Four Just Men ingeniously murdered a cabinet minister in Downing Street, in the Edgar Wallace thriller.

The embryonic ideas for the London of the future lay, many of them, housed in the Festival site, on the south bank of the Thames between Waterloo and Hungerford Bridges. Weary of war and its aftermath of austerity, shortages, rationing and never-ending queues, the nation was bent on a spree and flocked to see the prospects of a brave new world. Patriotism was the flavour of that wet English summer. Every conceivable article from tea cosies to carrier bags was red, white and blue, and Jennifer, on a routine visit to the dentist, had had her teeth gratuitously polished to give what she was told was a Festival Smile. Dylan Thomas at the time dubbed London the 'Capital Punishment', but he loved the Festival. This was a strange moonscape: the huge, steel-skinned, inverted saucer of the Dome of Discovery; the squat Shot Tower, which had always been there but somehow hitherto escaped notice; and, dominating all, the symmetrical stick-insect shape of the tall Skylon, a vertical javelin epitomizing new thinking, a new, higher yardstick of design in everything, incorporating (ominously significant to the doubters) no visible means of support and deliberately built-in obsolescence. By night, seen from the Embankment, it looked like a floating fairyland.

By the time we were able to visit, early in the school holidays, the Festival was nearly three months old and there was some excitement as the five millionth visitor, expected to clock in at any moment, was due to get some magnificent prize – I forget what. A gaudily decorated 'Bailey' bridge had been built alongside Hungerford Bridge from Charing Cross Underground (now Embankment) for pedestrians, and we spaced ourselves out along the extensive queue to increase our chances of hitting the jackpot. It was ten shillings for admission, which was a tidy sum then – rather more than the return fare from Eastbourne. None of us won any prize. Jennifer thought we should demand a recount. To get our bearings, we made for the centre of the complex, where there was a scale model of the Crystal Palace, centrepiece of the previous exhibition a century before. Erected, we discovered, as an afterthought at the last moment, the model remained there long after Dome and Skylon had gone, and was the last thing to be dismantled.

Instructive it all was, but also supremely festive. There was so much – too much – instruction: history, science, literature, geography, art and architecture; but it is the décor and the trivia that remain clearly in my memory's eye. After all, we had just escaped from four months of solid instruction. Conspicuously, there were no aspects of strife, but an emphasis on 'British contributions to world civilization in the arts of peace', as I think the mouthful put it. It was possible – maybe advisable – to follow suggested routes through the various pavilions, imbibing in articulate sequence orderly draughts of British farming through the ages, British geology, British technical achievement or the ascent of the Briton from the Stone Age; we, however, careless of edification and beguiled by the colour and inconsequential detail, wandered where the fancy took us and gulped at random.

Everything was new, futuristic and slightly hysterical. Everywhere was unfamiliar pre-stressed concrete in unexpected, fly-away shapes, painted in pastel shades: pale ochres, greens, blues and beiges, and every tone of pink. Festival Rock (the edible stuff – the music had yet to be invented) sold at 1/1d a stick (plus sweet coupons!) – 'just over 5p today – striped in red, white and blue with the Festival Device, an attenuated four-point star topped by the helmed head of Britannia, going all the way through the centre. This was the beginning of a time of thoughtless iconoclasm for all aspects of Victoriana. What though the modernism was brash? Sweep away the old, dictated the mood, and on with the new! It is easy to be critical with hindsight, to complain that it should have been apparent that much of the structure and design was as evanescent as the intriguing little whirling mobiles that ornamented the bridges, but new-born revolutions do not pause to wonder how permanent is the future they are so eagerly heralding.

Modern ideas in their infancy filled the pavilions. Theatrical lighting effects illuminated towering rubber plants and open stair-cases – what somebody called the 'marriage of the utility with the romantic'. Much of the Dome combined planetary Dan Dare land-scape with designs based surrealistically on atomic structure (the atom was a new mystery), florid nuclei encircled by bright whizzing electrons. The murals of John Minton, soon to die prematurely and unnecessarily but not quite as cruelly young as Tim, made a con-siderable impression on him and were greatly to influence his style. Outside, surprises ambushed the visitor round every corner. Here lurked a Henry Moore figure, a smooth hole where the abdomen should be ('That reminds me,' gasped Jackie, 'have we remembered the sandwiches?'), and there a pastel wall with a column of spread hands scaling it illogically.

Art seemed to have lost all credibility. A popular attraction was a huge water sculpture built of cascading buckets which pivoted, teetering, and emptied one into another and clanked like the armour of the White Knight – a tall equestrian model of whom spoke to a model Alice, complete with model image, either side of an imaginary looking glass in the entrance to the Lion and Unicorn Pavilion. Their conversation was audible on a looped tape as you went in, though curiously it was not from Lewis Carroll's text. In the Shot Tower, lead shot was once manufactured by dropping the molten metal through perforated holes in a sieve at the top, the drops solidifying during their fall to the bottom. Now it was mounted with a radio telescope dish aerial and sent signals to the moon which could be heard reflected back after two and a half seconds. Small beer today, but I believe it was instrumental in the building of Jodrell Bank.

In the Country Pavilion I was on more familiar ground. Birds and mammals of the British Isles lived captive behind glass in realistic habitats. Milk was displayed in all its stages from country pasture to urban morning cornflakes, at one end on hoof inside a four-strong dairy herd, at the other safely delivered into the bottle. On a huge plaster oak tree intertwining with an ascending staircase was a huge plaster Garden Tiger moth. There was even a big 'Live Butterfly Window', an entrancing sight, though by the end of July it was not home to as many species as I was told were present in the peak butterfly months of May and June.

The 'Tekkinema' survives as the National Film Theatre, which at any rate is more comfortable to pronounce. Here we were introduced to a marvel of the age, the 3D film. We were told it would soon be the regular thing, but somehow it doesn't seem to have caught on. At the door we were issued with special spectacles. The programme started with predictable gimmicks: an express train roaring up the auditorium; a man in a toyshop batting a ball on elastic all over the place. There were some restful abstract cartoons, in which worms of colour interlaced fantastically to music, followed by Vincent Price in *The House of Wax*. I suppose the extra dimension must have added a macabre lustre to Mr Price dunking unfortunate girls in a cauldron of piping wax. I do know that for some time afterwards Tim would jump out at us from dark corners, face atwist and body awry in horrendous parody, and limp off, cackling horribly. We were relieved when he went back to his Noël Coward imitations.

Considering how much of the past is vivid in my memory, it is surprising, though possibly eloquent, how little of consequence remains of the Festival. The South Bank Exhibition faded with the summer, as it was destined to do, an 'insubstantial pageant' to 'leave not a wrack behind'. Two wracks I know were left behind: the Festival Hall and a relic of the new designs, those metal-plastic stacking chairs which are found in all village halls today and are quite impossible to use as a piano stool.

About three miles upstream, just south of Chelsea Reach in Battersea Park, the truly festive, frankly uninformative side of the Festival Coin had emerged. Here a new-minted funfair and Pleasure Gardens combined the romance of one-time Vauxhall with the ebullient bravura of Derby Day and 'Appy 'Ampstead – even, I dare say, of the Fair of Bartholomew. It was a never-land pastiche of tree walk in the foliage and toffee apples on the fairground, disorientating crazy house, dizzy big dipper and a Mississippi showboat (Festival of *where*?), its paddles crazily churning the air, and a whizzing octopus of revolving cars which shot you insanely into a water splash. And noise. Noise from the bandstand and noise from the insistent, asthmatic steam organs; noise from the barking stall-holders and noise from the sensation greedy, goldfish-winning crowds; hot dogs, helter-skelter and hoop-la; dartboards and dodgems; ghost train, living tableaux and tunnel of love, and, for those with the stomach for it, nauseous-looking cumuli of red, white and blue candy floss.

We visited Battersea more regularly than its sober partner on the South Bank, ostensibly because the entrance fee was a mere six-pence. Such economy was deceptive, for each short-lived attraction at the funfair required a further coin, but hilarity counts no cost. Our favourite diversion was the Rotor. You climbed up a spiral staircase inside a vertical tower and looked down on a huge revolving drum. In this cylinder people were whirling, stuck to the wall like flies, twenty feet up, by centrifugal force. It looked fearsome as the drum accelerated and the floor fell away beneath them. Nervous onlookers could escape to the outside without having to pay, but we were game for anything. The sensation was surprising, though, versed as I was in the behaviour of the semi-circular canals, I suppose I should have expected it: there was no awareness of movement. As the drum picked up speed, you felt yourself tilted on to your back and lay heavily horizontal. Beyond the top of your head was a spinning maelstrom of spectators. The unbelievable part was the sight of other members of the party apparently glued to the ceiling directly above. Once in this rubber-lined barrel you could stay for as many spins as your churning insides could tolerate. So addictive did we find the sport that the management came eventually to recognize us and let us in free, 'pour encourager les autres'.

Two of the best things in the Pleasure Gardens, consistent with what we are told of the best things in life, were free. Promptly on the hour the crowds would converge on one point to watch the chiming of the Guinness Clock. Wheels, hemispheres and hammers, birds and mannikins whirred, rose, fell and spun in logical, if non-sensical, sequence to announce the time. The second, even more grotesquely appealing attraction was the sight of the engines, rolling stock and railway, built life-size from the drawings of Roland Emmett in *Punch*. The Far Tottering and Oyster Creek Railway brought his cobwebby and strangely sad phantasms to eccentric life. An emergency kit contained matches and kindling wood. 'IN CASE OF FIRE: Break glass, remove Contents and Light Fire in Fire Engine'. Platforms were loud with notices. A luggage crane, a hybrid born of a bird cage and a mangle, bore the stern legend, 'It is forbidden to wind other people's luggage up and down'. Other rules were more peremptory: 'Do not tease the engines'; 'Do not feed the bats' (this in the entrance to the tunnel), and, supremely, the unequivocal 'IT IS FORBIDDEN!'.

On our return, flopping exhausted into couch and armchairs, we would launch into the platitudes game.

'Well, here we are then.'

'Yes, that's about it then.'

'That more or less wraps it up' . . .

Hesitation or repitition counted you out, and the one who could sustain the flow of stultifying remarks longest duly won. Our entertainment was largely of the do-it-yourself variety.

Tim would seat himself with an enormous drawing-board, while we gathered round him, and build intricate, labyrinthine story sequences which he called 'films'. These invariably featured Spot, an imaginary dog with an evil eye who was to be seen later in many of his cartoons and illustrations. Such impromptu epics in which we all appeared, falling off cliffs or floundering in the sea, appropriate dialogue encapsulated in balloons, were the forerunners of the work he was to develop on *That Was the Week That Was*. They had important titles, such as 'War in That Dog's Field', and hiding in odd corners were eloquent beetles and moles, or a little flower which announced, 'I am very "smorl" and weak!' That 'smorl' had us in stitches, for no reason I can think of. I still have his 'Birds of South Ruislip, a survey conducted by T. Birdsall'. It depicts such feathered gems as 'The Small Moses: not so small as *some* birds, it is none the less smaller than the Large Moses, which is greater in size.' There is 'The Brown Chap: a proud bird whose eerie call, "Have you rung up the furniture people yet?", is one of the delights of the hedgerow.' And 'Purbeck's Collapse: this breed is fast becoming extinct due to its inability to fly. A fool on the wing.'

A craze for Square Dancing came and went, and, with a makeshift compass of chalk and string, we marked out broad areas of material to be cut into ample discs by the girls. These they made into swirling circular skirts, worn over an effervescent froth of lacy petticoats. We made do with check shirts and conventional grey flannels, with of course turn-ups, for jeans had not yet crossed the Atlantic. Neither, indeed, had the term 'teenager'. Youth had not the particular status that it was soon to claim. We were 'adolescents', which was some-thing of a put-down. Any assertion of personality would be explained away complacently by my mother with 'It's all right – he's going through a stage.'

Apart from the perennial singing and our home orchestra, and for me of course the moths and butterflies, our main preoccupation centred round a puppet theatre. Into the shows were channelled all our various skills and talents, including my mother's. Sculpture and dressmaking, electrics and scene painting, stage management and script writing, and of necessity the delicate art of manipulating the intricate strings. We worked on a scale of two inches to the foot. Many of the numbers relied on gramophone records. Our cabinet gramophone was of the wind-up sort, but we adapted it with a crystal pick-up head and used our pre-war Phillips wireless as a speaker. Coloured lamps and 'gels' furnished an efficient lighting system, battens, floods and footlights, and in an Eastbourne junk-shop we happened on a sturdy rheostat which made an effective dimmer. Sally envied this refinement and came bluntly to the point, as was her custom, one day over lunch at Knowle House. 'Could we have a dimmer, Daddy?' Her father unhesitatingly pronounced that in his considered opinion she couldn't possibly have a dimmer Daddy than the one she'd got already, and the matter was shelved.

Puppet making is the nearest mortals can get to realizing the ambition of Pygmalion, for each marionette takes on traits and a personality of its own, and not only when it is in action on the stage. An empty theatre is an eerie place at the best of times. An empty puppet theatre, with the whole repertory company hanging behind and watching you silently in the gloom, has an even more awesome creepiness. When the curtain rises, however, to a mood of expectant gaiety, the excitement is intense, blending backstage all the joy, the jokes, the pangs, the despair and the triumph of the real thing, confined within the space of a broom cupboard.

Our first character was the creation of Patrick – he still has him – a bizarre figure in motley, cap and bells, tersely christened 'Clowney'. His very ugliness caused Tim and me to doubt the wisdom of bringing him on, but we hated to disappoint Patrick and of course, from his first entry, he stole every show. Apart from his solo turns ('Popo the Puppet', 'How much is that Doggy in the Window?') Clowney compèred every performance and was always ready to improvise at a moment's notice when accidents happened. A carelessly dropped puppet meant an hour spent later, disentangling strings. Most numbers were conventional enough – the Laughing Policeman, the Little Dutch Mill, Waiting for Henry Lee, and splendid settings for ensembles such as Polly Perkins and Pedro the Fisherman. Jennifer and Sally guided a dying ballerina who rose from her bed to partner a skeletal Dark Angel through a chilling *danse macabre* to Sibelius's *Valse Triste*, an enchanted item and the most serious piece to grace our repertoire. Patrick devised a little old man whose neck and body were a 'cello and who played himself, scraping the bow across his tummy. How to play such an off-beat character? In a flash of inspiration Tim dug out a worn violin record of the Barcarolle from *The Tales of Hoffman*, so scratched that the background sounded like a rainstorm on a tin roof. So 'Cello Man played his mournful dirge to a theatre queue in a downpour with aching pathos. He was indescribably funny. On a good night we would get coins thrown on to the stage.

At Christmas time we used to stage a hastily written romp of a pantomime, when all the familiar characters put on different hats and took part. It owed much, I confess, to the then innovatory surrealism of the *Goon Show*. Clowney, like Harlequin of the previous century, always played the lead, in spectacular feasts such as 'Clowney Half-Whittington and his Resourceful Feline Companion' (the latter was a favourite in 'I T'ought I Taw a Puddy-Tat'). Late in 1952 we presented our most ambitious venture, the whole of *Trial by Jury*, the culmination of almost a year's head-carving, body-building and costume-cutting, with a cast of some thirty puppets. The two choruses, bridesmaids and jurymen, were cleverly strung so as to move in unison, each group worked by one person. Short gaps in the action were unavoidable as the piece demanded a pile of eight records, but we now had an electric gramophone and Charles eventually had things working remarkably smoothly.

The previous summer Jennifer had been on a visit to Sedbergh with her parents and had insisted on my escorting her up Winder on a hot June afternoon. We duly scaled the mountain and returned to tea in my study – an unprecedented event for which I had asked no permission. On the way out, as the sky suddenly opened to a drenching cloudburst, we met Michael Thornely. I introduced Jennifer and he, blandly incurious, lent her his umbrella to get back to her hotel. A year or so later they were married and lived happily ever after. In 1953 we gave our last series of performances of 'Trial', this time joined by Michael, who added the five guinea touches to rehearsals and, wonder of wonders, with a new long-playing record. No more gaps. The show was a pronounced success. Soon afterwards we were to move on, I to Cambridge and Jennifer to the London Royal Academy of Music, as the old records gave way to the long-players and the London trams finally stopped.

9

The Riddle
of the Sphinx

Privet Hawk caterpillar

OF THE SIXTY-FOUR DIVERSE FAMILIES WHICH MAKE UP OUR TWO thousand or so species of British Moths, none is so striking as the family *Sphingidae*, the Hawk moths. The name Sphinx was probably suggested by the sturdy, smooth-skinned caterpillars and their statuesque immobility of attitude when at rest, with a hooded head raised and pointed forwards, and a robust, erect horn curving backwards at the tail end. 'Hawk' refers to the moths. They all hover with wings beating at very high speed, rarely settling but, thrusting long tongues down into nectar-filled trumpets, seemingly motionless. They are streamlined, built for speed – and look it. Their forewings are long and pointed, the hindwings relatively small and rounded. Their bodies, thick, often colourfully banded and tapering to a point, extend well below the hindwings. The Sphinxes are mostly late dusk fliers, and there is a whiff of nocturnal mystery about them which we found fascinating. They are very much moths of the southern counties, for they are at their most active on warm, velvet nights.

The Lime Hawk moth has a wingspan of from two and a half to three inches. A background of greyish pink is relieved by broken bands and borders of dark olive green, a pretty combination and one that the moth uses to good effect. The outer margins of the wings are irregularly scalloped, and when at rest the moth so arranges its wings that the hind ones protrude sideways beyond the forewings, giving an imitation of a bunch of young leaves. We would find them in the afternoon, resting on a fence post or the trunk of a lime tree. A row of pollard lime trees stood outside Mr Cannon the Cobbler's shop in our Hertfordshire village, and a fine lime grew in our Eastbourne garden. On one occasion a beautiful Lime Hawk, surprisingly undamaged, was brought in by the cat. The caterpillar, fairly stout but tapering towards a triangular head, is a pale lime green roughened with tiny yellow pimples. Oblique yellow stripes shaded with dark green run parallel to the line of the rear horn, and together they look like the veins and stalk of the underside of a curled leaf. These caterpillars, so well camouflaged by day, stood out among those that shone up clearly in torchlight at night.

The Poplar Hawk, which for a long time as children we misread as the 'Popular' Hawk, is somewhat larger than the Lime. It is rather dowdy, a dusty grey brown like a faded tapestry. In the old days the Great North Road was bordered either side by two spiring lines of 'Cobbly Trees'. This was my childish attempt at pronouncing Lombardy Poplars, and the name stuck. I would stare longingly at the trees as they rushed past, wishing we could stop, thinking what wealth of Poplar Hawk caterpillars must be there for the taking! In fact, though most species of poplar are host to the Poplar Hawk, I don't think they favour the Lombardy variety. We never stopped to find out.

Nor did we stop at another curious landmark, which we called, a little unimaginatively, the Funny House. It was densely covered in brightly painted, carved models: sun, moon and stars, scrambling people, animals, birds and insects, a pair of giraffes framing the porch and a stiff-legged stork topping the lot on the chimney stack. Why the house was there, what bizarre humour had prompted the artist to spend his life peopling his walls with so extensive and capricious a pastiche, remains a mystery. Craning at the car windows we would stare out as the house flashed by, avid to spot a new piece of the jigsaw to add to the composite picture of what we had already established. The fragmentary glimpses made it all the more exciting. It may still be there – I don't know. It is all bypassed now and I prefer to cherish the memory.

The Poplar Hawk is one of the two Hawk moths which I occasionally come across in Yorkshire. A few years back Wendy and I were disturbed nightly by a scuttering behind a wardrobe, one of those insistent little noises which sound exaggeratedly loud when you are trying to woo sleep in the small hours. Convinced it was a mouse, after the third restless night I hauled out the wardrobe from the wall. Testy and indignant (why had I taken so long?) out flew a female Poplar Hawk moth, pollen damaged but still very active. These moths often come into the light, huge and alarming if you don't know them, and she must have stayed the night and got trapped. I released her near a poplar tree the next evening.

We would sometimes find the eggs when searching poplar or sallow trees, but, as is usual with the Hawk moths, rarely more than two on a leaf. Mostly we would search for the caterpillars in August, and would find them motionless and inscrutable. This big caterpillar is green and stippled with yellow points, the oblique stripes pale yellow. The head is a rounded triangle and the horn a darkish green with a yellow stripe, important points of identification as it has a close and similar cousin which also favours the same food plants.

If you see a caterpillar that looks identical at first, but has a triangular head that is pointed at the top and a horn with a tinge of blue, then it will be an Eyed Hawk. The roughening stipples tend to be whitish, giving the wearer a slightly frosted appearance. Interestingly, the

Eyed Hawk caterpillar reverses the normal cryptic shading, being paler above than below. It prefers to sit upside down on a twig. If you search for the Eyed Hawk at night you have to shine the torch downwards from above. We found one or two every year on Great Aunt Ethel's apple tree.

The moth itself is a very lovely one. The forewings are a greyish pink, marked with waves and patches of chocolate brown, merged like the shadows and highlights on brown velvet. The hindwings are a rosy pink, with a pair of prominent 'eyes', painted with a slate-grey pupil, pale blue iris and a broad kohl fringe of deep black. Disturbed at rest, the moth will draw its forewings slowly forwards and reveal this startling pair of eyes, a basilisk glare.

The Hawk moth which we found in the greatest numbers was the large, handsome Privet Hawk. It is not, in fact, as common as the three I have already mentioned, but we devised a highly efficient method of discovering the caterpillars. The moths can often be seen in a southern garden at dusk on warm June nights, hovering round the honeysuckle, where you can hear the vibration of soft wings, or picked out by car headlights at the strong scented flowers of wild privet in country hedgerows. The tips of the narrow, swift forewings can span well over four inches. These are a mottled, pale brown, shaded lengthways with black as if stroked with charcoal and merging to pink at the outer edges. The head is pink, the back blackish with white badger stripes alongside, and the abdomen, save for a central pale line down to match the forewings when they are folded, is boldly banded across with pink and black. Add two coral pink hindwings with broad, charcoal bands and you have what is a very fetching ensemble. It is rather wasted in the dusky gloom, the wings beating so fast that the result is no more than a blur.

The Privet Hawk caterpillar must, I am convinced, have served as a model for the grouchy one which Alice met, though I confess I have never seen one sitting on a mushroom. Nor for that matter smoking a hookah. He is big, around four inches in length when fully grown and as thick as a finger, a pale, translucent, smooth green with a shiny black and yellow horn and oblique stripes of lilac-purple, edged with white. In spite of this apparently gaudy costume, he is very difficult to spot. He sits motionless during the day, assuredly the most sphinx-like of the family, his front half raised and his chin tucked down over his legs which are folded together forwards as if in prayer.

For the record, I have found Privet Hawk caterpillars feeding on the wayfaring tree and on guelder rose, but their staple diet is privet. Privet hedges were rife in the Eastbourne gardens, growing above walls of buff grey brick and flint, straggling over pavements of well trodden red brick. A newly hatched caterpillar is about a quarter of an inch in length if you discount the horn, which at this stage is rather more than half the length of its tiny body. As it has to reach full size in the space of some seven weeks, it has an enormous amount of feeding to do. When mature it will strip whole stems bare overnight. In Hertfordshire the old farm-hands knew the caterpillars as 'locusts'. Obviously such big eaters will produce a commensurate amount of excreta.

Unpleasant though the subject may sound, caterpillar dung (known as 'frass' to the trade) is dry and odourless. Cleaning out the floor of a cage is easily done with a dry paintbrush. Once you have seen one caterpillar turd you might imagine you've seen the lot, but far from it. The stools of the Hawk moths are patterned and indented like a pineapple; those of the Privet like a hard, black little Mills bomb. These, in August and early September, we would look for at the inner edge of the pavements, eyes down as we walked along. A tell-tale scattering betrayed the presence of a caterpillar on the hedge directly above. All we had to do was to stare at each stalk in turn until we spotted him.

When the Privet Hawk caterpillar is full grown it takes on a brown tinge as though stained with tobacco juice. Maybe this is what gave Lewis Carroll the idea of the hookah. It becomes very restless, a marked contrast to its normally stolid, sphingid behaviour. It will wander many yards away from the foodplant and burrow into the ground, often to a depth of two or three feet, and there hollow out a chamber, fragilely shored with silk, where it finally changes into a large, shiny brown chrysalis. As soon as a caterpillar 'browned' and went walkabout, we used to transfer it to a box filled with peat. Each caterpillar would march round and round the box for about half a day and then disappear 'underground'. The moths hatched out the following June.

Although I have stated that the Hawk moths prefer the sunny south, the two rarest to come into my hands were both found at Sedbergh in the hardy north. One of these was the ominously named Death's Head Hawk moth. This is the largest of our moths. There is one other which matches its wingspan, a full five inches in the female, but the body of the Death's Head is stouter, as thick as your thumb. Appropriately enough, the huge caterpillar feeds on deadly nightshade, though it will also eat the leaves of the related potato. They were familiar to one or two old hands who worked in the potato fields in Hertfordshire, and who called it the 'Tater Hawk'. The labourers would pick them up and drop them, for, traditionally, a larva once handled would soon die. Such smatterings of folklore would make me wildly envious, for I have never seen one.

My moth has forewings of a brown, slaty blue, suffused with patches of golden ochre which look like irregular highlights and disguise the shape. Jagged lines of black cross the wings, meeting transversely when the wings are folded at rest to give an appearance of rough bark, a rich, dark brocade. The head and body are of the same slate blue, the stout abdomen is boldly banded with tiger stripes of black and yellow, and the hindwings, broader than those of most of the Hawks, are the same yellow with notched, black bands. On the back of the thorax, sinister and startling, is a distinct gold skull-and-crossbones. This beauty came to me in September 1951, when I was summoned during evening prep by Mrs Bruce Lockhart, who had recognized it for what it was. Some men had been replacing a stout gatepost, and as the old one was hauled out, the moth flew out lazily, apparently from the hole. As I transferred it to a collecting box it squeaked like a mouse, which may sound like a surprising reaction from a moth, but, from my reading, I knew it was not to be entirely unexpected.

The uncanny, staring skull emblem had, in older, more superstitious times, branded this moth as a foreboder of pestilence and death. Moses Harris, the eighteenth-century lepidopterist, called it the Bee Tyger Hawk moth. Certainly the moth has an authentic history as a robber of the old, straw skep beehives. I don't think the modern hives would provide space for access to such a large intruder. Its unusual squeak is held to emulate the queen and keep the bees happy while it sups its fill. Gilbert White noticed the squeak, recording on 11 October 1777 'a little, stridulous noise'. He called it 'a noble insect of vast size'.

The other vast and noble Hawk is the Convolvulus Hawk, as long in the wing but narrower in the body. It is rather grey and drab, except on the abdomen where black and pink bands are relieved with white like a faded cricket blazer. My only capture of the moth was in mistake for a large Privet Hawk. I was returning to my rooms in Christ's College, Cambridge late one evening when I spotted it hovering over a patch of petunias. I ran to collect my net and hurried back to find it still busy there. Only when I got it into the light did I realize what a prize I had taken. The Convolvulus has a tongue of prodigious length, perfectly suited to reaching into petunias and nicotiana. Once known as the Bindweed Hawk, appropriately enough, it was also called the Unicorn Hawk. As the caterpillar's single horn is common to the whole family, I imagine it was the notable tongue that prompted the name. I set mine with the coiled tongue extended, just under four inches in length. It is the champion hoverer of them all. In spite of the rapidity of the wing-beats, it backed and advanced precisely, thrusting its extended tongue into each flower in turn in an almost leisurely manner. It reminded me of something my grandfather said while we were watching a cob swan displaying on the Round Dam in Skipton Woods. 'Look at that stately, majestic glide! Under the water where you can't see, those little feet are churning away like all hell!'

I had met the Convolvulus Hawk a decade earlier, in connection with a much scarcer Hawk moth. As this rarity is not in my collection I have no locality label to fix the date, but it must have been the summer of 1942 or 1943. The locality was the searchlight in the village, and the searchlight was gone by 1944. The powerful light attracted moths in their hundreds. I would not want you to think that the local battery was hampered in its efforts to pin-point enemy aircraft by small boys cavorting about with butterfly nets. Moths unable to escape the magnetic beam will creep into some sheltering crevice nearby and hole up for the day. Our searches took place in the morning, stoically tolerated by the soldiers who stood around in braces and shirt-sleeves, faces usually covered in shaving soap. It was my friend Brian who, with an eager whoop, found the Bedstraw Hawk moth.

The moth is an olive brown in the main, with a broad creamy white stripe running diagonally to the tip of each forewing and a broad cream patch on the hindwings with a flash of rose pink. We took the moth to the Rector for positive identification. He was quite excited. I think there had been only one record in Hertfordshire, back in the 1880s, and he had none in his extensive collection. He offered Brian, then about ten years old, a big Convolvulus Hawk as a swop. The Bedstraw is little over half the size, and the exchange was made with satisfaction on both sides.

I captured a similar Hawk moth in the June of 1949, the other rare Hawk which I found at Sedbergh – and which I still have. The Striped Hawk moth is broadly like the Bedstraw, a little larger and the cream suffused with pink, the colour most in vogue with the family as a whole. The name derives from the veins of the forewings which are picked out in white, giving the striped appearance. 'Aunt' West had come to visit me in my first summer term and I had taken her up Frost Row to see my hide and the curlew nest. I was, unusually, quite unprepared, having neither net nor collecting box, and spotted the moth low down on the turf. Luckily West had a cigarette packet and gallantly emptied the contents loose into her handbag. I could find only one Yorkshire record of the moth, in 1868. What made the find of even more interest was that the beautiful moth, on being transferred to the packet, squirted a copious splash of bright pink fluid, a certain indication that it had just emerged from the chrysalis. This was no recent migrant, but had actually been bred on the Sedbergh fell. The caterpillar feeds, like its cousin, on the 'lady's bedstraw', which grew in the area.

Fashionably pink, the pinkest of the family, are the two Elephant Hawk moths. The Large Elephant Hawk which is fairly well distributed in the north though much more common in the southern counties, has forewings of greenish olive with two pink stripes, shaded with dark olive, slanting towards the wing-tips, giving it an impeccably svelte look. The body is deep pink with olive green and sharply pointed at the tail. The hindwings, black at the base, are the same glowing pink, smartly offset with a narrow white fringe. It is the loveliest of our Hawk moths. It is not jumbo sized. The name derives from the caterpillar, which tapers to a trunk shape behind the head and has painted 'eyes' and whitish stripes reminiscent of tusks. The moth was one of the prizes when we were night mothing on the edge of Sinjun's Wood, and it would be lured either to a sugar patch on a tree trunk or to a light. Patrick, who farmed for a bit near Wetherby in Yorkshire after leaving school, reared a caterpillar in his digs. Unfortunately it escaped from the breeding cage when it developed its pre-pupal wanderlust and his short-sighted landlady found it on the stair carpet. Thinking 't'wretched dog had done it', she picked it up on a shovel and flushed it unceremoniously down the lavatory.

The Small Elephant Hawk, less than two inches in wingspan compared with the two and a half of the Large, sports the same deep pink, with a golden ochreous spread in the centre of the wings. Although it is not uncommon, I have not come across this pretty moth very often. I once found a young caterpillar on the Downs near Beachy Head while I was rummaging among the lady's bedstraw (the plant, I hasten to add). It is similar to its larger cousin except that it lacks the Hawk moth horn, making do with two raised pimples instead. I nursed and reared it, and it duly chrysalled up on the surface of the peat at the bottom of the cage, having spun a lacy, token cocoon. In those days I would keep overwintering chrysalids on cotton wool in perforated tins returning them to more spacious accommodation the next year for hatching out. The tins were kept in a shaving cabinet in my bedroom, presumably once a maid's milk-safe, for it was open to the fresh air at the back, protected by a metal gauze screen, a highly suitable place for my purpose. This chrysalis, I remember, was in one of those useful, square red tins in which Messrs Benson and Hedges used to purvey their rather up-market cigarettes. Some time in early spring I took out the tin to examine it. I was horrified to see a long brown centipede, in frantic haste, slither out from under the closed lid. I couldn't believe there was room for it to squeeze through, but sure enough it had just been breakfasting on Small Elephant Hawk and my chrysalis was dead. How the centipede had known there were pickings there and considered them worth a two-storey climb up an outside wall was a mystery.

The two remaining Hawk moths hovering around my memory are small, chunky day fliers, enjoying strong sunshine. The Humming Bird Hawk moth is an immigrant from the Continent, though it is reputed to hibernate here, and occasional records of it very early in the year seem to give credence to the theory. In two or three hot summers of my boyhood it was extremely common on the south coast in July and August. Although all the Hawk moths behave tolerably like humming-birds, the robust body of this particular Hawk relative to its short, narrow forewings – an inch and three quarters from tip to tip, a quarter of this span is comprised by its broad back – probably comes nearest to the humming-bird shape and gives it the most rightful claim to the title. In addition, the body, which extends for half its length beyond the hindwings, is trimmed with feathery tufts of white and black. The forewings are grey, with narrow, waved, black transverse lines, and the small hindwings are orange.

The Humming Bird Hawk was a veritable 'towny' and led us to trespass on formal municipal flower-beds, especially where petunias and asters were in evidence. Patrick would get from various agents helpful intelligence of big moths seen in the ornamental gardens, notably a husband and wife team who supervised the adjacent Ladies' and Gents' on the promenade and used to appear alternately at the doors for a breath of fresh air like the figures in a weather house. (We fancied they had spent a lifetime in the trade, from Birmingham to Bermondsey, and had achieved a lifetime ambition, retiring to a white-tiled dream cottage at the seaside for their twilight years.) The Humming Bird Hawks were no easy catch for, although seemingly intent on their business, shifting quickly a few inches to pause suspended at each flower, if the slightest disturbance betrayed one's approach they would dart off at tremendous speed. Unlike most moths, rain never seemed to deter them. On days when nets would have been reduced to soggy swabs, we have seen them unconcernedly visiting the flowers in a steady downpour.

The Bee Hawk moths look rather like bumble-bees, with clear transparent wings, in shape very like the Humming Bird Hawk. They do not behave like bumble-bees, however, neither buzzing nor bumbling, but dart and hover in the family fashion. Tim caught our only specimen of the Broad Bordered Bee Hawk moth. It is so called because the four clear wings are edged with brown borders, and, like his 'Small Moses', the Broad Bordered Bee Hawk has borders which are broader than the borders of the Narrow Bordered Bee Hawk, which are narrower in width. The flowers which the Broad like best are the trumpets of rhododendron. As our normal habitats were predominantly chalky, the shrubs were not abundant. Tim was in London when he made his catch, whiling away the time waiting for Dad, who was visiting the Central Middlesex Hospital in north London, and saw numbers of Bee Hawks visiting the flowers. Having no net with him, he managed with consummate skill to catch one in a handkerchief.

I spotted one years later, on the outskirts of Abbot's Wood in Sussex, where it was hovering over low-growing bugle flowers, unmistakably a Bee Hawk. As I failed to catch it, I cannot comment on the breadth of the borders. From the habitat I suspect it might have been the Narrow Bordered Bee Hawk.

There are four other Hawk moths which I have never seen alive, all rarities. The Pine Hawk is a resident, the other three are for the most part immigrants: the Spurge and the Silver Striped Hawk moths, both similar to the Bedstraw, and the magnificent green and silver Oleander Hawk moth, a very rare visitor from Africa. Even Watkins and Doncaster, I recall, had only one of these. Much has yet to be learnt about the migration of moths, and many of the visitors are less at risk than our indigenous residents from the depredations of our agriculture and development. The true riddle of the Sphinx is that these beauties may crop up anywhere unexpectedly, a delight to those with the experience to recognize them. All moth enthusiasts are reputedly mad, but, like Hamlet, 'I am mad nor-nor-west; when the wind is southerly, I know a Hawk from a handsaw.'

10

Juvenes Dum Sumus

Christ's College, Cambridge

Mʏ ENTRY TO CAMBRIDGE IN 1953 WAS CLOUDED BY NONE OF the mistrust which had characterized the two previous plunges into new routine. I knew lovely old Christ's College of old, as my father had often taken us round throughout our boyhood, and since the age of sixteen I had made visits to sit various parts of the 1st MB examination, stepping-stones to a career in Medicine. My final visit had been the year before, to try for a choral scholarship which in the event I did not get.

Auditions were held in King's College, in the sumptuous rooms of the renowned Boris Ord, whose reputation for irascibility was, I understood, on a par with his musical one. I arrived at the ante-room to join a handful of wary contestants, all smart and scrubbed. We were checked and marshalled by a nervous Dean with a clipboard who danced in with each retreating candidate and disappeared on tiptoe with the next. The last on the list before lunch, I was left alone while a rather blasé young god went in before me to be put through his paces. I could hear him begin his scales in a confident baritone. He was stopped abruptly by a discordant crash from the piano. 'Sing "LA" – not "LOR"!', came a stentorian snarl in the persuasive tones of Charles Laughton on the quarter-deck of HMS *Bounty*. The scales continued less confidently, and my last vestiges of morale seeped away through the soles of my shoes.

I had always accepted that ornaments should not be placed on the top of the piano, as they produce unwanted vibrations. It was a day of shattered precepts. On entering the big room I was dimly conscious of black gowned figures, like a parliament of rooks; dons, tutors and college organists, perched round the boundary on window seats and antique chairs. In the centre was an enormous grand, every available square inch of its surface reflecting a sea of tiny, exquisite porcelain figurines. Wildly inconsequent, my first thought was that it must take the proverbial seven maids to dust here every morning. In astounding contrast, at the business end sat the huge Boris Ord, sagging, mottled and amphibian, his hands like bunches of bananas floating over the keyboard in a series of delicate arpeggios. He thought it was time to knock off for lunch.

I survived ear tests and scales (to a carefully articulated 'LA') without mishap, the key ever rising sadistically like the bar of the high-jump. The Dean tripped forward with a manuscript, and I looked at it. No bar lines or time signature; square, mediaeval notation – it might have been the Rosetta Stone. Really! I wasn't aiming at the King's Choir. Just an unpretentious little Sunday job in the Christ's chapel. Furthermore, the words were in Latin with an English translation underneath. Did they favour veni, vidi, vici, or the passé weeny, weedy and weakie? I was hanged if I was going to be caught out on pronunciation. With a hopeless prayer I launched into the thing in good, honest English. A palpable wince ruffled the rooks, and up fussed the dancing Dean. Would I sing it in Latin? Deliverance came from an unexpected ally. 'Let the boy sing in English,' growled Boris, the genial, sympathetic maestro. 'I don't understand bloody Latin either!'

The Cambridge I loved devotedly in the mid-1950s, changed superficially today, had altered little since my father's time. C.P. Snow, himself once a Junior Fellow of Christ's, described it succinctly as a 'mixture of luxury and bizarre discomfort'. There was a pervasive smell of gas from 'Ascot' heaters combined with a yeasty whiff in the Screens from crusty bread and ancient, beer-steeped floorboards as you passed the cramped old Buttery. Gas today is not as smelly, and the Buttery is now a smart bar in oak-raftered rooms which I once knew well, but a few paces from the busy street past the Porters' Lodge (the Head Porter whom I knew was so tall, handsome and distinguished in his top hat that most visitors took him for the Master if not the Vice-Chancellor himself) still takes one into a First Court of poignant beauty where the centuries fall quietly away. It was an inspiration to me then, and is now, that if the poet, Milton, had been dropped by some celestial parachute into First Court, he would have been instantly at home in his old College.

Milton had been suckled here and, defiant legend has it, planted a mulberry tree which still survives. His young portrait still hangs in Hall, with the flowing golden locks which earned him the title (which he repudiated most unpoetically) of 'First Lady of Christ's'. Wordsworth first got drunk in Milton's rooms on a visit to a friend who occupied them nearly two centuries later:

> O temperate Bard! . . . I poured out
> Libations, to thy memory drank, till pride
> And gratitude grew dizzy in a brain
> Never excited by the fumes of wine
> Before that hour, or since.

One hundred and forty years were to elapse before Sam Birdsall had the self-same rooms. His libations were poured no less convivially, but with rather greater frequency.

Milton, epic poet, was also to my delight capable of lighter stuff as an undergraduate. The now proverbial Hobson, the carrier, kept his livery stables just round the corner and died at the grand old age of ninety. He had hired out forty hackney horses but as, to ensure a rotation, only the one near the door was ready, saddled and bridled, the hirer made do with 'Hobson's Choice'. He had started his business before Shakespeare was born. As the young Milton wrote:

> Here lies old Hobson: Death has broke his girt,
> And here, alas! hath laid him in the dirt. . . .
> If any ask for him, it shall be said,
> 'Hobson hath supped, and's newly gone to bed.'

Charles Stuart Calverley, poet and wit, moved here, sensibly, from Oxford. His odes were to beer and tobacco. Once, showing a friend round, he tossed a pebble at a window, and remarked, 'That is the Master's window.' 'And that,' he continued on the appearance of an enraged face, 'is the Master himself!' Charles Darwin mounted beautiful plaques (for his maternal forebears were the Wedgwoods) to decorate his rooms, and they still do. At Christ's he was an avid collector of beetles. On one occasion he had found a prize beetle and spotted another making its escape. Typically, such a windfall happens when one is without a collecting box. To leave his hands free he popped the first one into his mouth, whereupon it 'exuded acridity' and he promptly spat it out again.

In the mid-twentieth century there was still a primitive scarcity of baths and lavatories. The city was thronged of a morning by young men in dressing-gowns with towels round their necks on their way to a distant tub. Christ's College boasted three courts, and in a corner of the second a stone outbuilding had been converted into a six-stalled urinal known to the inmates unofficially as Fourth Court. Roger Thompson, architect in embryo, executed a fine plan of the College which was framed outside the Porters' Lodge. In it, unremarked or at least unerased by authority, Fourth Court, to general approval and amusement, was given official title and status, and greatly bewildered the visitors who, naturally, could never find it. At a recent sunny, alfresco reunion we found to our (literal) relief that Fourth Court was still there. It had been extended to incorporate a Ladies' wing. Opinions differed whether this innovation should constitute the Court of Appeal or, alternatively, the Court of Petty Sessions.

Cambridge undergraduates were then mostly more mature than today's counterparts, in experience if not necessarily in deportment.

The last of the wartime ex-servicemen had 'gone down' – and a lively bunch they had been – but National Service claimed the majority before University, so the average age was two years older than the norm. This showed itself especially in sport, where the added years of development at a critical period made a robust difference. As a medical student I had been deferred for National Service. Most of my friends, far from sampling the first tastes of the cakes and ale, were already seasoned campaigners determined to enjoy their new freedom to the full. Surprisingly maybe, the old rules were never questioned, but in time-honoured fashion were ingeniously circumvented. Gate fines were still operative after ten o'clock, though often endowed by anonymous donors – I never found out how or why – and after midnight, when College was locked, we climbed in – or out – over walls fortified with broken bottles and barbed wire. We would not have had it any other way.

Two particular friends had only just survived the war in Korea. Neither talked about it much, but such proximity to their own deaths had left them with an inner stillness underlying the youth and high spirits which I am sure they were quite unaware of. I have met this aura a few times since in people who have suffered great privation, most recently in the adorable Hannah Hauxwell, whom my wife and I were privileged to meet, though privilege is a term which would puzzle her. Her tranquillity flows from her, born of a far from tranquil loneliness, struggling by herself with a smallholding on the stern slopes of the northern Yorkshire Dales. Such people do not swear in rage, as you or I do, when a shoelace breaks. Admittedly, one of my friends had only one shoelace to bother about.

John Whybrow had come into abrupt contact with a hurled grenade. As it rolled towards them he ordered his men back to safety and promptly 'fell on the ball'. John had been a promising athlete. With a pair of crutches and his remaining leg he used to leap through the courts with twelve-foot bounds, brought back to me in startling recollection by a recent performance of *Richard III*. As darkness fell he could be heard outside in Third Court, rending the quiet fortissimo, in a passable imitation of Sergeant-Major Britten. 'Monopeds – ON PARADE! LEFT, LEFT, left-left-LEFFFT!'

John was fitted with a temporary, stiff wooden leg, discarded his crutches and walked with a stout stick. Soon he threw that away as well. Only occasionally, returning from a Saturday evening's inspection of the Cambridge hostelries, would he lean heavily on one's shoulder, making no comment and expecting none. Eventually came a sophisticated, life-like prosthetic limb. John danced, even rode a bicycle. He became so adept with this new, light leg that it was undetectable. He would raise his right leg to the horizontal and lower himself to the ground and up again, perfectly balanced, and challenge anybody else to do the same. Source of many simply won pints. His most disturbing trick was casually to roll up his trouser leg and stub his cigarette out on his ankle.

Ben Moore had been shot through the lungs. He had been rushed to an American base hospital. Here the 'bull' of the British equivalent was tempered with mercy. Patients in bed were not expected to sit or lie 'to attention' during the visits of higher ranking personnel. There were, however, unlooked-for hazards. Ben was in constant trouble through habitually addressing nursing officers as 'Sister'. Ignorant that the term was a title of rank and dignity in the hospitals of the Old World, his ministering angels of the New felt that the unfortunate soubriquet was altogether too familiar. One day a brass-hatted general came round the ward distributing 'purple hearts', the medals awarded to all Americans who are wounded in the service of their country. Ben duly received his, but some officious spoil-sport denounced him as an English usurper and the general came and took it back. A shame, as it was a trophy he would have loved.

The only advice my father gave me prior to my going up to Cambridge was, above all, make a friend of your Gyp. The Gyp was the man who maintained the residents' rooms on the staircase, woke you up in the morning with a strong cup of tea, cleaned your shoes, made your bed, swept and dusted your quarters, furnished you with up-to-date College gossip and, with luck, was a mine of information ranging from cautionary advice to cures for a hangover. A mixture of Sam Weller and the Inimitable Jeeves. The female equivalent, of which there were then only a few, were known ambiguously as Bedders. 'Aut Senex aut Horrida', insisted the University Statutes – either old men or horrid women – though to my knowledge none of the cheerful ladies conformed to this prescription.

Cyril, my personal guardian angel, was a painter, and we would discuss his latest work brought in with the morning tea. Literary, too, was his bent, and he lent me a book, *A College Mystery*, which told the intriguing story of the Christ's College Ghost, one Christopher Round, who walked the Fellows' Garden on summer nights in the May term. The tale is authentically associated with early experiments in anaesthesia in the last century, and explains why the eventual credit went from Cambridge to Edinburgh, but it is too long to tell here. Cyril was a chain-smoker, a drooping cigarette perpetually wobbling on his lip as he chatted, and though I left a profusion of ashtrays, which he cleaned assiduously, he would always empty his own ash on to an open hand and rub it down the ample front of his apron, which developed a grey, dusty patina like the breast of a pouter pigeon. The Gyps, though we did not know it, were the last of their generation. Many had grown old in the service of the College and had known my father in his day. A sign of the changed times was that then they had been known by their surnames, whereas we addressed them by their Christian names.

Sporting prowess alone was no longer a qualification for entry to Cambridge, though not a few of the dons felt aggrievedly that it still was. Brawn had to be tempered with a modicum of brains. A precise and calculated balance was achieved in Christ's by the redoubtable Dr Pratt, the Senior Tutor, who shrewdly weighed every candidate seeking admission. A benign Machiavelli, brilliant physiologist, brusque and blunt with a searing, cynical wit, he saw penetratingly into the souls of the young men whom he ruled. A classic story was told by the late Jimmy Harrison of his first interview with Pratt, his ability on the rugger field clearly having gone before him. He knocked tentatively and, at the customary bellow of 'Come!', opened the door. A rugby ball came at him from nowhere like a bullet, and he instinctively turned and took it cleanly. 'Right, you're in. What's your name?' I saw more of the Senior Tutor than many and viewed him with more affection, for he was my tutor in physiology and a group of us used to meet him once a week in 'supervisions', a demanding taskmaster but a hilarious companion. His face was disfigured by an unsightly naevus but, such was the personality of the man, one rarely noticed it.

Medicine as a subject for study is as potent a draught as any medicine in the pharmacopoeia. Although most medical students arrived damp-eared from school, the two-year lag in maturity was precipitately bridged by the uncompromisingly practical nature of the work. No doctor will forget his first sight of the dissection rooms. At the age of nineteen few have had any direct contact with death. A schoolfellow, Neil McShane, who was to be my partner in all practical work throughout our university days, had discussed the event with me beforehand into the small hours. We were more concerned with our behaviour than with the initiation itself. Having donned immaculate white coats (the sure badge of the neophyte) in the locker-room, we entered together. Before the scene had had time to impress me, I found Neil had turned a livid shade and now fled in panic, leaving me to face the ordeal alone.

Neil's rooms in Pembroke were conveniently near. I found him a little later, rebuilding his shattered nerve with brandy and coffee, which he conjured noisily like a mediaeval alchemist with the aid of a decrepit Cona apparatus. 'Never, never again! I can't go through with it!' These dramatic turnabouts were an integral part of Neil's constant upheaval of a life. An excess of liquor or love invariably moved him violently to forswear for ever the contributory factors, and as regularly the same restorative would redress the balance. Once, in our schooldays, a 1st XV away match fell on a Friday the 13th. With exuberant defiance, Neil crossed his knives at breakfast, spilt salt at random, trod on spiders, left pins scornfully where they lay and walked provocatively under any ladder he could find. During the match he had a leg broken in six places. Thereafter he was the most superstitious man I ever knew. I persuaded him to return to the dissection rooms without further incident.

In fact, though forty or so cadavers lay on high, glass-topped trolleys in the spacious room with its quiet, cathedral-like atmosphere, they had an air of unreality and seemed like effigies made out of grey plasticine. They were protected by the same 'sleeve' as I remembered on the carcases at Smithfield meat market, which jolted me to a sense of our commonplace mortality and pointed some kind of a confused moral. I felt no queasiness and little fear, only a ridiculous dread that among these lifeless models might lie, impossibly, someone whom I recognized, to explode the myth into terrifying truth. It was only much later, at my first post-mortem, that I experienced the faintness, and that again was at the commonplace: the familiar, clean scent of fresh offal on the butcher's slab, emphasizing our undeniable kindred with the beasts of the field.

As the year progressed and each subject was gradually whittled away by half a dozen pairs of students working on different sections, discarded bits were carefully kept together and in due time given a suitably reverent interment away from our ken. Fred, one of a pair of lab assistants, little, old and bent, with a wry face pock-marked like the craters of the moon, kept up a scavenging routine around the dissection rooms with a swab and a broom. Subjects for dissection came from varied sources; a very few had bequeathed their bodies to science, others were vagrants, destitutes from the workhouses and the occasional suicide. Naturally no details were available, only the age and cause of death, but for the latter the significant 'carbon monoxide poisoning' told its own sorry tale. When Neil and I were dissecting the head-and-neck, our subject was a little, emaciated tramp who had died of exposure and malnutrition. When we trepanned the skull, that is removed the top to reveal the brain below, the protective membranes were covered in a green layer of mildew. Our first indication that Fred was also a witness of this disturbing find was an incredulous voice between our shoulders. 'Gawd, sirs! 'E must 'ave 'ad a dirty mind!'

The boisterous behaviour of medical students as a species has been well chronicled throughout the ages. Much of it is a reaction to the unequivocally grave nature of their studies. Lectures were intense, but relieved by touches of real humour. (I recall arriving five minutes late at Barts for a lecture by the tyrannical Yorkshireman and great anatomist, Professor Cave. 'I'm sorry I'm late, sir. Tubes were slow.' 'Well, take more roughage and sit down!') Most pranks were unmalicious and taken in good part. Lack of a reciprocal sense of humour was the undoing of the earnest lecturer. One unfortunate Australian physiologist, brilliant in his field but tediously dry in delivery, complained bitterly of the constant late arrivals to his nine o'clock instruction. Any more of it and he would cease to appear. He hid his irritation when, the following day, his audience arrived prompt to the minute in dressing-gowns and pyjamas. Half an hour later, on the appearance of cornflakes and bottles of milk, his patience snapped and he stalked out amid cheers. During his final lecture in the May term, a sack was opened to release a justifiably indignant goose. It immediately identified the speaker as the source of its woes and belligerently went for him, to be fended off by the alarmed academic with a long blackboard pole. The Marx Brothers had little to offer in comparison.

By no means did we have it all our own way. Dr Pratt was dealing with the physiology of diabetes. He held up an amber filled beaker. 'This is a sample of diabetic urine. You will appreciate,' he said, stirring the contents with a finger and then sucking noisily, 'that it is distinctly sweet to the taste.' He handed it to the nearest occupant of the lowest of the benches, a wide bank of which rose in raked, semi-circular tiers to the back of the hall. The beaker was tested and passed from hand to hand, from tier to tier. 'Is it sweet?' I asked Neil. 'Horribly!' he grimaced. I passed it quickly to my neighbour 'As future doctors,' continued Pratt, when the depleted beaker was returned to him, 'you will require to be observant. No doubt you perceived that the finger I dipped in the specimen' – once again he waggled his forefinger in the sample – 'was not the one I sucked.' Ostentatiously he put his middle finger in his mouth and his tongue firmly in his cheek.

Conspicuous by his height among our year's batch of medics was a young Jonathan Miller, a shock of red hair prominent above a shabby, navy-blue fisherman's jersey, and his extraordinary prehensile feet habitually bare. Undoubtedly one of the most brilliant among his contemporaries, he was known more widely in Cambridge as a humourist. His mobile face had an india rubber quality, with a lower lip that protruded like that of a bactrian camel which he could consummately imitate in a supreme series of animal mimes. 'Just imagine you're a black beetle!' – and he would virtually become one. He did spindly drawings for *Punch* and in those days before the Fringe and the Establishment was very much a one-man show. I have an abiding memory of him at the end of one term, setting off for London on foot – barefoot as usual – his belongings in a canvas gunny-sack trailing behind him on the end of a long rope held over his shoulder.

Seen with hindsight, in the mid Fifties the retort was beginning to bubble with the effervescent reaction between the old and established and the new and experimental. I must have been one of the last of the accepting generation. Even the sixteen months separating the ages of Tim and myself seem now to bridge the gulf between the acquiescent and the rebels. Conformity was maintained to a certain extent by the two University Proctors, one of whom would tour the city at night with his two henchmen, culled from the college porters, known as Bulldogs. They made a Dickensian picture, the Proctor in flowing gown, mortar-board, hood and tabs, his bullers in frock coats, with their top hats secured to their collars in case of attack. One Bulldog was chosen for his bulk, the other for his fleetness of foot.

My sole brush with the Proctor (in the dark I had failed to see the trio approaching) was for the crime of smoking in academic dress. My gown, the wearing of which was mandatory in the streets after dusk, was rather tattered and also came in for criticism. Such encounters were marked by extreme politeness. A day or so later a card arrived in my pigeon-hole inviting me to call on the Junior Proctor in his rooms. In panic I realized I had done nothing about my gown. No friend was available to lend me one, and I spent a frantic half hour with safety pins and a clothes brush. Proctorial fines were always a multiple of one-third of a pound, and my two offences clocked up thirteen shillings and fourpence. 'The new gown is something of an improvement, Mr Birdsall. It may console you to know that the late King George VI was also "progged" for smoking.' On a later confrontation, Neil and I were escorting an old school friend, Bob Rhodes-James, now Conservative Member for Cambridge, who was over on a visit from The Other Place. He was not wearing a gown, had no need of one away from Oxford, but a Bulldog was speedily sent over to us. The top hat was courteously raised.

'Excuse me, sir, are you a member of the University?'

'I am,' boomed Robert orotundly, 'a member of *The* University.'

'Thank you, sir.' Once again the topper was doffed. 'Good evening!'

One major portent of the iconoclasm to come, an obsession incomprehensible to our parents' generation, was our cult following of a new comedy series, *The Goon Show*. Conversation was studded with 'cardboard replicas' and 'Have a gorilla!' and Eccles and Bluebottle were mimicked to excess. It was the zany, surrealist humour which appealed, rather than the underlying snooks cocked at The Old Guard. Be that as it may, private radio sets were rare, and owners would find their rooms crammed at seven-thirty on a Thursday night, for a sacrosanct hour in the weekly timetable. Television had not yet invaded the Colleges. There was a vogue for rambling, Heath Robinson VHF kits and a few men had new, upright, bulky tape recorders. Typically, the first experiment with this innovatory machine was to swear into it – could that unfamiliar voice really be one's own? – and the second was to leave it on during a party. Unlike the versatile human ear, however, the microphone was unable to beam in selectively on an individual and the results were always unintelligible.

Barriers were being broken in other fields too. In 1954 Roger Bannister ran the first sub-four-minute mile. On a rare visit to a political meeting, I heard Rab Butler, then Chancellor, state that the standard of living would double within the next twenty-five years. It seemed a long time. The Alexandra Palace opened in Cambridge. This was one of the soup kitchens, furnished with peasant austerity, avant garde in décor and economical for frugal pockets, which were soon to evolve into the ubiquitous espresso coffee bars, birthplaces of 'skiffle' groups and the pop culture to come. Authority kept a watchful eye on the university publications, especially the remarkably professional *Varsity*, the weekly newspaper, and the more upmarket magazine, *Granta*. Occasionally one or other would be suppressed by the Proctor, when feature or criticism overstepped the accepted bounds of taste or permitted comment. Prominent among contributors were the late Nicholas Tomalin, Michael Frayn and Bamber Gascoigne, the two latter to overlap and collaborate with Tim.

The Old Guard still kept a firm hand on the helm, and felt secure enough in its supremacy to be tolerantly benign. All scripts had then still to be vetted and passed for public performance by the Lord Chamberlain. I would throw in a few deliberate gaffes for the blue pencil, hoping to draw attention away from more subtle effrontery. Kenneth Tynan's 'salivating monster' was dormant, not to rear up with discordant menace until *Look Back in Anger*, when the decade had passed the half-way mark. Still, inexorably, the retort fizzed, throwing up to the surface, as happens at such times, discrete lumps of the reactive ingredients. Popular imagination harked back to the Twenties, a period, relative to the end of a world war, strongly analogous to our own, and the novels of Angus Wilson had a nostalgic vogue. Witty, tuneful revue, still typified by the current *Airs on a Shoe String* and the stylishly satirical *Lyric Revues* at Hammersmith, was jolted by the futuristic *Kranks*, where smoothness was discarded. Taste swung away from the big American musicals towards light, home-grown pieces. Sandy Wilson's *The Boy Friend* (timely parody of *The Girl Friend* in which our Aunt Sheelagh had appeared) started at the Players' Theatre Club as a wistful romp, caught the fashionable rage for the Twenties and transferred with enormous success to the West End. Even more successful, breaking the record run for a musical held for a generation by *Chu Chin Chow*, was ex-Footlights Julian Slade's whimsical, melodic *Salad Days*. I went three times with friends to see this delectable, frothy fantasy, and each time danced from the Vaudeville to King's Cross on the journey back to Cambridge.

The pioneering ripples which announced the threatening waves of change were not so discernible in Cambridge itself, which remained aloof and detached, much as it had always done. The pubs, now alas a vanished world, preserved in the main a placid balance between Town and Gown, providing recreation and refreshment in equal proportions. The Pickerel near Magdalene Bridge is the only one of my regular haunts still to survive. Erik and Muriel Frieman, who kept it then, will remain in the memories of hundreds of Cambridge graduates when the names of their dons are mostly forgotten. Many a sporting giant, among them one who is, at the time of writing, steering the MCC in the current struggle for the Ashes, left his pewter tankard to decorate the ancient beams which threatened Erik's head. For he was built like a mountain, like his Viking ancestors, though his weapon was slightly less warlike: a large carving knife which he wielded with dexterity on vast, cold joints of lamb, pork and rare roast beef. Ten brimming pint pots, five in each hand, he could carry with cheerful ease. Muriel, with a voice like emery paper, could be a tartar. A self-appointed deputy mother to all her regular undergraduates, her wrath at any infringement of manners or stupid conduct — and everything got back to her — was formidable. Once faced, however, it was soon over. If the ratio of strong ale to study became out of balance, Muriel would bar the offender for a prescribed time.

The local characters in the Pickerel were legion, but my favourite was little 'Orace, who stood about knee high to the landlord. The 'tweeny' of Magdalene College, he could be seen crossing between the kitchens and Hall, staggering under a pile of plates half as tall again as he was. Friendly patrons in the bar would remove his flat cap, rub his bald pate for luck and replace the lid.

''Morning, sir. 'Ow are you?'

'Good morning, 'Orace. I'm very well. How are you?'

'Now that's very nice of you, sir! I'll 'ave a mild.'

Little 'Orace's eventual demise was a characteristic little tragedy. He rode a child's bicycle. One day in Milton Road he was overhauled and run down by a double-decker bus. The anguished driver hadn't seen him.

From the Pickerel, where I lunched regularly, I could reach the medical schools by an almost direct diagonal line, on ancient rights of way which passed through various narrow passages and three pubs. The Blue Boar was an old coaching inn opposite the Trinity gateway where, if you look carefully, Bluff King Hal still holds a chair leg to replace a sceptre purloined long ago. 'The Pig' as it was familiarly known (one night its snarling heraldic sign was transformed with pink paint into a saucy little piglet) was the most central of the Cambridge hotels, and though expensive it kept a good cellar and the meals were excellent. Bert, the head waiter, was bland and imperturbable. He had a well-known trick of producing the right overcoat for a departing guest. This once so impressed a visiting bishop that he quizzed him. 'How did you know that was my coat?' 'I don't, my lord,' replied Bert, 'but it is the one you brought in.'

Next on the route was another coaching inn, the Lion in Petty Cury, nicknamed 'The Leo'. You will still find Lion Yard, but the whole is now a huge, modern shopping complex. The old inns had been converted to twentieth-century requirements by the relatively simple expedient of glazing over the inner courtyards. In the Leo the massive old oak gates still stood at the street entrance, as in the Colleges, with a small wicket door giving access when the main doors were shut. Within, rooms, bars and stairs off were still labelled with the old signs, 'Ostler', 'Boots' and such. The stable yard floor was carpeted and flanked by settees and tables along the whole of its length. The manager was large, florid and not excessively genial, but then no doubt his nature had been sorely tried on many occasions by his often raucous clientele. He seemed constantly on the alert for some fresh outrage.

He had a small, compact corgi dog who had just the same temper as his master. A friend of mine, Michael Fann, had a smouldering feud with Mine Host which was taken on in turn by the dog. One day we were sitting on one of the courtyard settees, quietly downing what Dick Swiveller would have termed a 'modest quencher', and the corgi came in from the street carrying a paper bag. It waddled down the length of the lounge seemingly oblivious. Opposite us it stopped, put down the paper bag with deliberation, trotted over to Mike, bit him in the ankle in an experimental way, returned to the paper bag, picked it up and continued on its course. This route continued to be used as a right of way, and unwitting diners, quietly sipping their coffee in the lounge, would often be startled to see a gowned cyclist pedalling slowly along the carpet in front of them to disappear at the far end.

Lastly on my route lay a hidden little Worthington house called The Bun Shop. Three draught Worthington brews were dispensed, the prestigious 'E' expensive at elevenpence the pint (in old money) and the lesser strengths at all of sevenpence. They were drawn by a motherly old soul called Mary and the luscious Olive, epitome of shapely young barmaids with a line of repartee more than able to cope with the crowd of Christ's men ogling her over the counter. The landlord, Les, had once toured the halls in a speciality act and on particularly festive evenings could be persuaded to do handstands balanced on a bicycle on the bar. This was the spiritual home of the Firkin Warbecks, one of those briefly mushrooming little College clubs which exist for no better reason than a good night out in convivial company, flourish for a few years and then die off as others takes their place.

Alongside rowing and revue and keeping an ever watchful eye for butterflies and moths, I spent a commensurate amount of time drawing and painting. There was no fine arts course at Cambridge, though art colleges were at the time proliferating country-wide, and artists were thin on the ground. This being so, I was in fairly regular demand as scene designer and illustrator. In particular I became involved in producing décor for the majority of the university balls. This started with the Christmas Ball of the Medical Society, but requests multiplied and I found myself the director of a companionable team dedicated to transforming at regular intervals the three floors of the Dorothy Café into forest glade, railway station, Hades or Olympus, and on one occasion the entire setting of *Alice in Wonderland* and *Through the Looking Glass*. Discos were unheard-of, and dance bands were still within the purses of the more affluent societies. This gave me a nodding acquaintance with bandleaders such as Geraldo and Nat Temple. Our fees were not excessive, in view of the work involved, culminating in an entire night spent in erecting the stuff, necessitating either an exeat on a trumped-up excuse or the customary scaling of the battlements before breakfast. Complimentary tickets for our crew was our reward, and a crate of Pimm's under our table with lemonade to taste. House champagne was prohibitive at the Dot, and girls would arrive like Agag, walking delicately, champagne bottles slung under their long dresses. Corkage was paid on one bottle, and thereafter the exempting label was transferred from one to the next while still wet.

One of the artists involved with our frivolous but necessary craft was Humphrey Boyle, whose epigrams and check trousers were famous at Cambridge at the time. His blond curls down to his collar, the Fauntleroy effect marred by a pair of quizzical, elderly spectacles, were conspicuous among a generation of short back and sides. Aesthete though he was, he was also an accomplished oar and, following his year as secretary, was elected Captain of Boats. He once stroked the first boat on a practice outing when an urchin fishing for sticklebacks shouted to his mate, 'Look! There's a girl in that boat!' On their return a couple of hours later, a crowd of small boys stood waiting. 'There you are!' cried the same voice triumphantly, 'I *told* you there was a girl in that boat!' Humphrey's art tended to the modern, and his methods to the eccentric. Against my advice he insisted on using the yolks of eggs rather than the whites to compound his tempera, spurning modern products. His rooms reeked of sulphuretted hydrogen like a mink farm. His parties were similarly bizarre. An old printed invitation, addressed to one James Birdlime and with 'Complimentary' scrawled across it, turned up in a box of assorted memorabilia.

> Mr. Lear, Mr. Whybrow and Boyle
> seeking rest from plumdomphious toil
> bid you come on the twelfth, and drink everyone's health
> and consume gosky patties in oil
> Please bring a runcible spoon.

Years later I visited him when he had taken on the family business (a fate to which he had sworn never to succumb) and was a prominent member of the local Junior Chamber of Commerce. Where were the dreams of youth? I need not have worried. Admiring a low wall he had built for seating round the open sitting-room fire, I commented on the bright, white mortar framing each red brick. 'Plaster of Paris?' I asked. 'No, no! Dental cement. Much cheaper!'

It was Humphrey who disinterred from a short abeyance the club which was nearer to my heart than any other, and with which I fittingly close the chapter on my days *in statu pupillari*. The Original Christian Minstrels were originally founded in 1867 by Alfred Scott Gatty, later Sir Alfred and Garter King of Arms, composer of, among other work, a series of exquisite plantation songs, now forgotten and, I think, unobtainable. Like me, Humphrey was second generation Christ's and had heard, as I had, glowing reports of the club from his father. The 'Christian' referred to Christ's College, though we were delighted, on advertising an annual dinner to old members in *The Times*, to receive a substantial discount as a religious society. The name was in fact a play on the Original Christie Minstrels, an American burnt-cork troupe run by George Christie which was enjoying wide popularity in this country in the 1860s, bringing to England the songs of Stephen Foster, such as 'Swanee River' and 'My Old Kentucky Home'. Well predating the Footlights, and one of the oldest surviving College clubs (only one other was permitted to sport the university crest on its badge and regalia), the OCM was limited to sixteen members and was founded for the enjoyment of good company, good wines and the ballads of the day. The wines gave place to beer but the ballads remained more or less of the day. Apart from original songs, little more recent than 1911 was permitted. The regalia was impressive, black velvet smoking jackets with intricate frogging, of which only three were to be seen in the club, handed down from fathers, among them my own. The colours of the braid and the bow ties had been chosen by the founder to tally with the name, and was an off-beat combination of orange, cerise and mauve.

As secretary and later president I was able to peruse the minutes at leisure, which survived miraculously from the foundation, handed on from scribe to scribe. They have now achieved special status in the College Library, where it is to be feared nobody ever looks at them. I noted that the spirit of nearly a century before was essentially similar to our own. Well-known names were there, among them the late Arthur Marshall in his day, and organ scholar Reginald Armitage, better known as Noel Gay, a minstrel if ever there was one, whose obituary we marked at a meeting in all solemnity with a slow rendering of 'The Lambeth Walk'. The old rules were pedantically adhered to. Meetings were candle lit. Smoking was not permitted, nor might the candles on the piano (which swung out on brackets) be lit until the minutes had been read. Words or gestures deemed unparliamentary were forbidden before the hour of ten o'clock, punishable by a fine, usually of candles. This kept the supply replenished. One night Ben prepaid for the evening with an altar candle of monstrous size. Whybrow was a talented accompanist, and Humphrey adept at the piano accordion. Members who were to achieve later acclaim included Gordon Clyde, who sang spurious folk-songs in bonnet and shawl, and Ted Taylor, who has written comedy scripts for the BBC ever since.

The OCM is a survivor. It had a few times in the past gone underground and been resurrected. It continued well past its blithe centenary but sleeps at the moment. I have sure faith that I shall yet attend another splendid dinner, though chorus and candlelight live now only in the memory. What choruses they were! How loud they still re-echo! 'Silver Threads', 'The Miner's Dream', 'Daisy', 'Lily' and 'Away Went Polly'; and the kilderkins rose gradually on their gantries till not a further drop could be coaxed out.

Gaudeamus igitur, Juvenes dum sumus: let us therefore rejoice while youth is yet with us. The final meeting of the May term, with its farewells to some and a welcome to others, culminated in a traditional dance of 'Nuts in May' on Third Court Lawn, when a hapless don (usually the Chaplain, the delightful John Brown) would be hauled out in his pyjamas to be 'pulled away'. Shortly after this ceremony, in 1956, exams over and somehow passed, I paraded with many others in the august panoply of a Bachelor of Arts in the Fellows' garden, awaiting the medieval ceremony in the Senate House. Dr Pratt was true to form. 'Good God! You here, Jimmy? I haven't been more surprised since Rita Hayworth married Ali Khan!'

11

Of Moths, Menageries, Maulsticks and Monologues

Red Underwing moths

M Y DAYS AT CAMBRIDGE WERE TOO CRAMMED TO GIVE MUCH time to the butterflies and moths, though I managed two or three expeditions to the Breckland and to Wicken Fen, two unspoilt tracts of habitat, differing from each other in their ecology and providing a refreshing change from university life when batteries needed recharging. Wicken I knew well from many visits during our childhood. It was here we had gone with my father for our first adventures in night mothing. Besides the lamp, which I have described earlier, a favourite pursuit was 'sugaring' at night. This was assisted in Wicken Fen by sugaring stations; slices of bark nailed on to posts at intervals down the cleared rides. The 'sugar' used was a mixture of molasses, coarse brown sugar and beer, boiled down to a sticky consistency and with a noggin of rum added for good measure. We applied it to tree trunks and posts with a paintbrush and inspected the patches in rotation with a torch. I still find it the most exciting method of attracting moths. One never knows what to expect. On the first occasion, in the fens, we painted our sugar in the afternoon, prior to returning at night. An early contretemps occurred when we lost the lid of the treacle tin. It had been placed carefully on a fallen trunk while we did the brushwork, but had completely vanished while our backs were turned. The mystery was solved when Tim, carrying the open tin with care, spotted the lid firmly glued to the seat of Patrick's trousers.

By 1955 the paths of my brothers and myself had diverged and the long holidays spent together, so long taken for granted, already belonged to the past. Tim was fast in the toils of the Royal Ordnance Corps which he suffered with an unmitigated, smouldering resentment, relieving his frustration with reams of ruefully funny, ironic drawings and caricatures which polished and refined his work to the knife-edge perception later to stand him in such good stead. Patrick had left school at sixteen and was farming in Yorkshire and later in Sussex prior to his call-up. I met up with Patrick on visits to my grandparents, and Tim and I coincided during his week-end leaves from the transit depot at Hounslow.

I was, thankfully, comparatively free during vacations, though bouts of study and the need for a holiday job – to raise funds for fees and buttery bill – interfered with my collecting expeditions, in prime moth and butterfly months which I had for years spent in the north. I used to spend days by myself with the net in hot, sunny weather, wandering the Ashdown Forest, the Downs and the cool environs of Abbot's Wood. A beautiful Leopard moth turned up under a beehive. I always gave beehives a cautious inspection for Death's Head

Hawks. I still do. Abbot's Wood yielded the Cream Spot Tiger, the loveliest and least garish of this gaudy family. Another large moth, its forewings are a deep black with broad spots of cream, the furry black and yellow body is tipped with scarlet, and the hindwings are pale yellow with black spots and blodges. On the edge of the forest I caught its little cousin, the Wood Tiger, who is dressed similarly in black and creamy yellow, and is a very fast daytime flier.

Huge moths are always the most exciting, though not necessarily the most elusive. In August, one of the largest, the Red Underwing, was not uncommon around Eastbourne, and could be found resting on willow trees near the railway line. On first sight when its wings are folded, it looks, apart from its size, like an ordinary 'mothy' sort of moth, a palish grey with jagged dark bands matching the tree bark. The hindwings, by contrast, are a deep plum red with a broad black splodge and border, edged with white like the peep of a petticoat. The sudden splash of colour as it starts to flutter probably has a warning effect to predators.

Holiday jobs between mothing – or rather combined with mothing, for I was always awake for the unpredictable – ranged from builder's labourer to barman and bus conductor. On most bank holidays I would go with a handful of my college friends to work in a small eleventh-century pub run by a delightful family, the Harbour Inn at Axmouth in South Devon. The work was demanding in the high holiday season, but I had a certain amount of time off for painting and for butterflies and moths which abounded on the sandy cliff tops, and quite a few prizes resulted. Many ludicrous incidents enlivened life among the bottles and barrels, and one in particular stands out in my memory, still causing me to prickle with shame. A customer was waiting at the bar, with a short, grizzled crop, collar and tie, eyeglass and hairy tweeds, and a pair of well-behaved Labradors on a double lead. 'Yes, sir, what can I get you?' A gruff bass asked for a large brandy and the siphon. I thought I detected a certain frostiness, but the military always made me uncomfortable. My discomfort was more acute when my customer moved away, to display a tweed skirt, thick woollen stockings and brogues below the jacket. It was my unfortunate introduction to a well-known lady novelist and broadcaster who lived at nearby Honiton.

My strangest job, which was near home and lasted a year or two with gaps, was painting scenery in a zoo. It was not a large zoo, and served no scientific purpose, but added to the attractions of a restaurant, children's playground and modest funfair. The animals were treated with kindness and affection, though rather cramped, and a coypu was advertised grandly as 'The Largest Rat in the World'. It was that kind of zoo. The proprietor was a Captain (RN retired) who still walked an imaginary bridge with ferocious eye, a daunting stereotype from the joyous comedies of Stephen King Hall. He was what in Yorkshire is known as 'careful'. On arriving for a day's work I would have either to vault the turnstile or pay the sixpence to get through. He would look in of a morning to check on my efforts, but I saw little of him save when I had to try and extract a fair price for a fair job done. He would outstare me incredulously, as he would a pink-faced midshipman asking permission to grow a beard. My constant companions were two real Sussex country folk, Bill the Thatcher, one of the few surviving craftsmen in his line as well as a general handyman, and 'Reeny', a warm-hearted former landgirl who fed and cleaned the inhabitants and still wore the uniform.

One day I rang my mother to say I had been bitten by one of the animals and was coming home early. I had been savaged by a wild fieldmouse. A wide glass-fronted cage was devoted to 'Mouse Town', where a colony of white mice disported themselves in a model village, with the usual little wire treadmills and other mouse diversions. I had to paint a funfair as a background, first removing the occupants to a temporary lodging. It was during this evacuation that the fieldmouse turned up, having, we discovered, gnawed his way in through an improvised back door. While I was restoring him to freedom, he, the ingrate, sank his rodent incisors into my thumb. Wild? He was probably furious. He must have had a rare old night, because after two or three weeks the albino coats of the inhabitants of Mouse Town, secure in their new, impregnable amusement park, showed a noticeable tendency to brown and white.

Two sizeable monkeys lived in large wire cages extending out-of-doors. Both were stimulating subjects for portraits, which I worked on when the coast was clear. A pair of squirrel monkeys stayed in their long cage with me and chirruped while I worked. I believe visitors thought I was part of the show. We certainly gave them their money's worth. I used to hold out the projecting end of a metal spring rule. One of the pair would grab it and dash off to the far end of the cage, extending it as it went. 'Nine foot three inches, thanks very much!' I'd say, giving the rule a tug so that it recoiled with a snap. This never failed to impress.

Often I was put through a catechism while I sketched and painted the backs of the cages, and I discovered prompt answers were more popular than long-winded authenticity. One lady pointed to a friend of mine who spent most of his life rattling around his cage, noisily shoving a heavy log about with his snout.

'What on earth is that?'

'I am told, madam, it is a porcupine.'

'Where does it come from?' (Were they never satisfied?)

'The Anchovy Islands off South America,' I replied without thinking. I found out later I had pinpointed the continent with laudable accuracy.

I was not really so casual. I genuinely did try to fit up the animals with their corresponding backgrounds, but the results did not always please either the occupants or my employer. Three marmosets, with tiny, old men's faces, were a constant delight, a never idle source of mischief. Their cage was double doored, so Bill built a temporary chicken wire partition inside to enable me to climb in and paint one half at a time, while the marmosets were secure in the other. This worked very well, provided I kept brushes beyond the reach of little hands, and I executed a mysterious, shadowy bamboo forest to make them feel at home. The Captain complained that it lacked bright colours. My explanation that their natural environment was a sombre one was neither here nor there. The marmosets' criticism was less explicit but more direct. The entire time I was painting beside them, the three little beggars made concerted dives for their water bowl, climbed the separating wire and continuously peed on me in relays.

During one week Charles and Sally were down with us, and Tim and Patrick were both at home. I did not want to miss the fun, so I brought home for painting, already measured and cut, sheets of hardboard, destined to enliven the cages of various parrots and other bright, tropical birds. Let the Captain have his colour, I decided generously. Bright, fecund jungle scenes resulted which would, for invention, have been the envy of a Douanier Rousseau, and we all took a hand. Landscape painting among Sussex chalk and Wharfedale limestone had left my palette with a preponderance of Indian red, raw Sienna and the rosier end of the spectrum, so, to use it all up, we invented a jungle weed called Firegrass which flourished luridly in every conceivable space. The colour-conscious Captain was loud in his approval.

Alas, my new-found popularity was later to wane. Tim was home on leave and used sometimes to come and collect me in the early evening, when we would go and enjoy a pint or two in the grand old smugglers' inn, the Star at Alfriston, before going home. Waiting for him, I would usually sketch in the rudiments of whatever scene I was engaged in the next day. On this occasion I was due to decorate the cage of a dozen guinea-pigs. I had been putting this one off, for it stumped me. Whatever is the correct natural habitat for guinea-pigs? I confided my worries to Tim. 'Medical research!' he exclaimed without hesitation and, grabbing my charcoal, drew with lightning speed a sketchy panorama of laboratory apparatus and white-coated, evil-eyed, devilishly grinning gentlemen waving hypo-dermic syringes. Laughing uproariously, we left for the pub.

Unusually, the Captain was waiting for me when I arrived the next morning.

'What the devil d'you call this?' He pointed apoplectically to the monstrous cartoon.

'It was a joke,' I stammered. 'It's not meant to be permanent.'

'Joke? Damn poor sort of joke! Don't know what you're thinking about. Anti-vivisectionists will be down on me like a ton of bricks! Scrub it out! What I want is something colourful!'

Now what, I asked myself angrily as the dust settled, can I do that is utterly, ludicrously incongruous? And colourful? With grim satisfac-tion I painted a Scottish loch. A castle sat reflected in the middle distance, heather and bracken glowed smugly in the glen, pine trees reared tall on the brae, and the distant blue mountains under a racing sky showed the silver of burn and waterfall. As I finished, I reckoned it had cost me my final fee, but the revenge was worth every meagre penny. Truculently I waited for the Captain to come and inspect my handiwork. He was delighted. Guinea-pigs took on a new persona for me. In their sublimely uncharacteristic setting they looked for all the world like roaming Highland cattle.

The Fifties moved on, and as we entered the second half of the decade, bastions were beginning to crumble more noticeably. Sir Winston Churchill, immortal old figurehead, had unbelievably retired from high office. The end of 1956 saw a return of petrol coupons and the final salvoes of the old Imperialist cannons in the Suez crisis and the abortive invasion of Egypt, culminating in the disappearance of another great wartime figure as Prime Minister Anthony Eden limped exhausted off the stage. Patrick went to Cyprus with the Royal West Kents. His experiences in this inflam-matory trouble-spot were to temper his sunny disposition for some few years, but his letters home gave little indication at the time. He did once write to me alarmingly: 'I am thinking of getting engaged to an Indian mud wrestler from Tel Aviv called Fingers Phyllis, but I can't decide between Partition or Union with Grease.'

Private T. Birdsall said his final farewell to the Army, with relief on both sides, and went on to Cambridge, where he made a prolific impact with his already mature cartoons and illustrations. By the time he 'came down' in June 1959 his talents had reached the notice of a wider circle, and he was offered a post by two national newspapers. The one he accepted was with *The Sunday Times*, for it wisely imposed no restrictions on other, freelance, work, provided it was not for a rival 'Sunday'. Here he drew the 'Little Cartoon' on the front page every week and illustrated features in more serious vein. The salary, at two thousand a year, was princely in those days for a young man on the threshold of his career.

This career was to blaze brightly for a brief four years, tragically to be extinguished by leukaemia. As Bernard Levin wrote at the time of Tim's death, 'It is not easy to be sure – there is so terribly little to go on – but I have always been convinced that, especially with the elaborate quasi-political cartoons of his last phase, Tim was developing into an artist fit to be compared one day not just with Low or Vicky, but with Daumier and Rowlandson, even Hogarth.'

Tim certainly combined a truthful economy of line in his drawing with a wonderful sense of fun and fantasy. He was appointed Political Cartoonist for *The Spectator* under Levin's editorship and it was here, and in *Private Eye*, that he did his best work in the genre; huge, baroque drawings with incredible detail. In one such, *Britain Gets Wythe Itte, 1963*, a satirical indictment of the already hysterical Swinging Sixties, beneath the hoardings and television cameras and placards ('It's New!'; 'Buye Something Todaye!'; 'Litigate!'; 'Thanks to Advertisinge!') and crowds of well-known faces, one can descry the accurate, intricate details of the environs of Trafalgar Square.

It wasn't all cartoon and caricature. Tim had ambitions to become recognized eventually as a serious painter. He sat in the Press Gallery in the House of Commons and produced some beautiful line portraits for *The Radio Times*. Of Macmillan, of course, but also many others. He loved drawing Bessie Braddock. These weren't caricatures, just straight drawings in his own mischievous style – and always with affection. He was disgusted with the more vicious satire. He drew all the Theatres of London for the Manders and Mitchenson book of that name, sitting out alongside the traffic. His output was enormous, almost as though something prompted him that his time was short – though he had, mercifully, no inkling of just how short, right up to the end.

To millions he was best known, of course, for his weekly spot on the Saturday night BBC television show, *That Was the Week That Was*, which erupted on the scene to stir troubled waters and ruffle establishment complacency late in 1962. Tim was at first worried by the controversial content of the programme but, as he told me, he knew that television would offer him an unguessed-at range for his drawings. In a few months he had, with his entertaining, analytic commentaries, quick pen and immediately likeable nature, given cartoons a new dimension that has never really been emulated since. He was of course a very handsome young man – the weight of his fan-mail testified more to that than to his art – but to Tim television was a means of developing his *métier*, and not a medium in which he wished to stay very long. He had no time for conceit.

For his family, the wit of his performance was often given extra spice by the background knowledge of how he had arrived at it. Patrick, after demob, spent some time with *The Daily Herald*, then, tired of London but not of life, took himself off to Australia, arriving in Melbourne with ten pounds in his pocket. After a year of hitch-hiking between adventurous jobs, ranging from Advertising Manager of *The Gippsland Times* to cane cutting on the breadline, he joined a geological expedition for a further year in the outback. He acquired a knowledge of the flora and fauna, the butterflies and moths, in areas which the majority of Australians never visit in their lives. Tim and I met him on his return at Victoria Station, with ten pounds in his pocket and a pronounced Australian twang, full of tales of antres vast and deserts idle.

Recollection is hazy. TW[3] was performed live, and not all programmes were recorded in those days. Ironically those that were owed it more to anxieties about libel action than to confidence about the future historic significance of the material. Tim's running commentaries, too, were breathlessly quick-fire. However, the week after the wanderer's return, Tim's routine had a familiar ring to it, spoken in impeccable 'Strine.

Timothy: That's an Australian painting. I'm an Australian painter – one of the best, Blue! I'm going to start at the beginning and give you a run down on the development of my work for the past thirty years. This is one of my early works (here he drew a horizontal line with his stridulous felt pen across the width of the large, blank board) –

'Landscape Northern Territory 1947'. This stresses the basic simplicity of Australian life – the sky and the land – the bare bones of Nature showing through. It has the advantage that you can't make a mistake and hang it upside down. You'd get a brown sky – and who wants a brown sky? I went on from there to something more complicated (an oval is drawn just above the line). 'Emu Egg Bouncing on Wire'. This illustrates a game played by the Aboriginal children in the outback. They bounce the emu's egg on the wire. And that's it. They're a very simple people. One from the history books here: 'The Story of Ned Sherrin the Famous Bandit'.
Shout from off camera: Kelly!
Timothy: Not right now, thanks! You see he's wearing a mask – to protect himself from kangaroo bites. Then I went on here to 'The Hitch-Hiker'. Another character in the Australian scene. (Two lines meet at the horizon in a big, inverted 'V'). Here we have the old devil there, Perspective, coming into play. We've not got much culture out here but a lot of perspective, so why not use it? I went on there to delve into 'Folk Lore and Legend'. There's the story of the man who fell hopelessly in love with a kangaroo and floated down the river with it to Melbourne where they both got arrested. A very bad story indeed. Anyway after that here we have 'Landscape with Telegraph Poles'. Illustrating the birth of the telegraph pole as a life cord in Australia, linking the people of the outback. They're seven hundred miles apart over there, you know, the telegraph poles. It's pretty tough out there with the sun beating down, flies drowning in your mouth, the wallabies running round in circles, five hundred miles to the nearest pub and only the bloody flying doctor to keep you in touch with civilization, it's a man's country, Sheila! (Here Tim reverted to his own voice.) So they tell me, anyway. I've never been there myself. I've got a little place in Chelsea, two up, two down, and who'd live anywhere else? . . .'

That's about it, then. Memories fade, but the moths, or many of them, still survive. Life has yet its surprises in store. A little while ago my wife and I, walking the dogs in a broad pasture on a warm, moonless July night near our Yorkshire village, witnessed the eerie dance of the Ghost moths. The male Ghost moth is a glaucous white, not luminous as we thought when we were children, but reflecting any light there may be. They had hatched out in hundreds from the roots of the grasses and were wavering slowly, vertically up and down about a yard from the ground as though each were suspended on elastic. The large, yellow-winged females fly up to them during this courting ritual and choose a mate. These ones had plenty to choose from. As far as we could see in all directions the air was full of the frail, white dancers. By morning they had vanished, every one.

'No man can truly be called an entomologist,' said Oliver Wendell Holmes. 'The subject is too vast for any single human intelligence to grasp.' He may be right, but it has been fun trying. Man is a natural pigeon-holer. I am sure that our cave-dwelling, Neanderthal ancestor sorted things into groups long before he could articulate their names. Cooking utensils would have gone in one corner, skins and bedding in another, hunting weapons handy by the entrance, and his favourite knapping flint on that ledge above the fire where the kids couldn't get at it. Identifying moths and butterflies spills over into other sciences, for no living group fits snugly into any one pigeon-hole. We became, without realizing it, involved with plants and flowers, with geology and chemistry and meteorology, with the whole complex ecology of the natural world and, inevitably, with our own kind. I am sure that conservation will only be maintained, not by the closing of footpaths, but by the opening of awareness and knowledge.

If my book can persuade one reader to rescue a moth from its frightened addiction to the light, rather than swatting it with a newspaper, perhaps to examine and even identify it before releasing it from the window of a darkened room, then my hours will not have been idly spent. For the fate of any species could well portend the eventual fate of our own. William Blake, in this as in everything two centuries ahead of his time, said,

> Kill not the moth or butterfly,
> For the last judgement draweth nigh.

And yet I can never feel that Blake derived any joy from Nature, which is the prime source of all good fun. Rather give me old King Lear, creation of that vast, wry humorist:

> We'll live, and pray and sing and tell old tales
> And laugh at gilded butterflies!

To which, with deference to Will Shakespeare, he might have added the moths.